The Strategy Playbook for Educational Leaders

This how-to resource provides leaders with a concrete framework for a strategic improvement plan, helping educators link the "principles" to "processes" of planning. Packed with key takeaways and additional resources, this book provides tools to design a strong strategy for improvement and enables educational leaders to think constructively about why we plan, what an effective strategic plan should contain, and how to create meaningful dialogue to support plan development, implementation, and monitoring for continuous improvement.

The Strategy Playbook for Educational Leaders provides superintendents, central office staff, principals, and teacher leaders with the opportunity to reframe the process of their strategic planning and breathe new life into the activity.

Isobel Stevenson is a Director at the Connecticut Center for School Change, USA. She has been a district Chief Academic Officer, Principal, Assistant Principal, Curriculum Coordinator, and Teacher.

Jennie M. Weiner is an Associate Professor of Educational Leadership at the University of Connecticut, USA. She has worked for Rhode Island Department of Education on issues of school turnaround and capacity building, and was a senior research associate for the Teacher Advancement Program (TAP) at the Milken Family Foundation.

Other Eye On Education Books Available from Routledge
(www.routledge.com/eyeoneducation)

The Strategy Playbook for Educational Leaders

Principles and Processes

Isobel Stevenson and
Jennie M. Weiner

Routledge
Taylor & Francis Group
NEW YORK AND LONDON

First published 2021
by Routledge
52 Vanderbilt Avenue, New York, NY 10017

and by Routledge
2 Park Square, Milton Park, Abingdon, Oxon, OX14 4RN

Routledge is an imprint of the Taylor & Francis Group, an informa business

© 2021 Taylor & Francis

Library of Congress Cataloging-in-Publication Data

Names: Stevenson, Isobel, author. | Weiner, Jennie M., author.
Title: The strategy playbook for educational leaders : principles and processes / Isobel Stevenson and Jennie M. Weiner.
Identifiers: LCCN 2020028417 (print) | LCCN 2020028418 (ebook) | ISBN 9780367313159 (hardback) | ISBN 9780367331702 (paperback) | ISBN 9780429318276 (ebook)
Subjects: LCSH: Educational leadership. | School improvement programs. | Educational planning. | Strategic planning.
Classification: LCC LB2805 .S7465 2021 (print) | LCC LB2805 (ebook) | DDC 371.2/011--dc23
LC record available at https://lccn.loc.gov/2020028417
LC ebook record available at https://lccn.loc.gov/2020028418

ISBN: 978-0-367-31315-9 (hbk)
ISBN: 978-0-367-33170-2 (pbk)
ISBN: 978-0-429-31827-6 (ebk)

Typeset in Optima
by SPi Global, India

Visit the eResources: www.routledge.com/9780367331702

For our children,

Manny, Rufus, Andrew, and Douglas

Contents

Preface

In one telling of the origin story of this book, it began in a Starbucks in Storrs, Connecticut, right opposite E. O. Smith High School. The two of us got together when, after showing up at many of the same meetings and saying very similar things, we realized we were interested in the same big ideas about schools and schooling. Even though we didn't know each other very well, it didn't take us long to decide that we were thought sisters and the ideas we collectively valued so much and worked so hard to engage with others should be captured and shared more broadly. We were going to write a book!

In another telling, this book began decades ago, when the two of us, thousands of miles apart, were each involved in writing and reviewing school and district plans. Our experience of this work was that the typical strategic plan in K–12 education was not doing what it was intended to do. The strategic plan, also known as the school or district improvement plan, or the continuous improvement plan, is supposed to lay out the actions that the school or district is going to take to fulfill its mission. Board decides on the vision, sets goals, writes a plan, and boom—achievement goes up, drop-out rate goes down, and everything's good, right?

Unfortunately, educational organizations often fail to live up to their plans' promises. The resulting explanations often include an all too familiar blame game – insipid goals, resistant teachers, lack of accountability, and lackluster leaders have all been trotted out as the reason why efforts fail. At the same time, we saw little reflection by those tasking schools and districts with engaging in planning regarding whether and to what degree current processes and approaches were necessary or appropriate. Time marched on, educators kept being blamed, and the approach to planning remained the same, despite the desire for different outcomes.

Educators bemoaned the fact that huge amounts of time and effort continued to go into producing enormous plans—pulling together data, consulting stakeholders, filling out templates—only to have the plans sit on shelves and nothing really change in the lives of students. Planning often became a dirty word, understood primarily as a compliance exercise more than a mechanism for real improvement and change.

We don't disagree that improvement plans have failed, on the whole, to live up to their name. But we don't think educators are to blame for these outcomes or that the solution is more ambitious goals, greater accountability, or more courageous leaders. We don't even think the solution is a better template. The revolutionary idea behind this book is that none of those things matters as much as a concerted effort to figure out what will truly make a difference in the lives of students, a method for capturing and communicating those ideas, and a way to continually modify practice to meet evolving needs. This is a book about creating the conditions necessary for continuous improvement.

Who Should Read This Book?

If your current planning process is working for you, that's wonderful—keep using it! But if you suspect that your current process is not delivering a good return on the investment of time and energy that you put into it, this book is for you.

In this way, this book is for educational leaders—including superintendents, central office staff, principals, and teacher leaders—who are perhaps dissatisfied with their current planning processes but unsure how to make them better. It is for leaders who want to find real and concrete tools to support a school system with greater equity, better systems (logic), increased coherence, and a focus on capacity building. We anticipate it would be the kind of book superintendents would share with teams of leaders, so they are all on the same page, so to speak, when it comes to restructuring or reinventing their planning practices.

What Will I Learn?

In this book we aim to share two key new learnings. First, we work to support leaders in developing a more complex and rich view of the possibilities of strategic planning. This includes challenging existing conceptions of the purpose of planning, how it should be implemented, and why. It also includes providing a clear and concrete structure, via our guiding principles, to support new understandings. Second, we provide new learning about the planning process. This includes asking school and district leaders to consider how they engage in their work together and if this is structured in ways that align with their goals. We provide concrete tools, including our Disciplined Strategy Map, and walk readers through their various components and how to work with your team to make these components best work for you and your specific context.

To facilitate these learning objectives the book is organized as follows.

Part 1: Setting the Stage (Chapters 1 and 2)

In this section, the focus is on unlearning current conceptions of strategic planning and creating new ways to conceptualize what the endeavor of strategic planning can and should be.

In Chapter 1 we introduce the big themes of the book and what makes Disciplined Strategic Planning different from traditional planning. We present and define our four big principles of Equity, Logic, Capacity, and Coherence, and how they guide the planning process.

Chapter 2 focuses on the intellectual core of the planning process: strategy. After studying many district and school documents over the years that were titled "strategic plan," the authors rarely saw a true strategy driving the proposed actions. Instead, many plans seemed oriented more toward fulfilling requirements for creating goals and action steps and less toward designing an approach to realize their aspirations. This chapter, then, is about strategy and how we might conceptualize it and use it for planning.

Part 2: Getting to Business (Chapters 3, 4, and 5)

Having built a shared understanding of Disciplined Strategic Planning, this part of the book is focused on how to engage in this process via the creation of a vision, a mission, and goals, and includes a number of tools to support these efforts and their relationship to leadership and instructional improvement.

Chapter 3 describes a new approach to creating strategy in practical terms and introduces the Disciplined Strategy Map to support this effort. It highlights the work necessary to create a strategy, along with tools to use during the process. The first steps are to create a vision, a mission, and goals. Next is the process of backward mapping to support the articulation of the plan. The chapter closes with an overview of how backward mapping supports the creation of a Disciplined Strategy Map.

Leadership and its relationship to strategic planning and implementation is the core focus of Chapter 4. Specifically, the chapter highlights the conditions that leaders in education—formal and informal—can create to enable the success of the strategy and to ensure it aligns with and is deeply rooted in the principles of Equity, Logic, Coherence, and Capacity.

It also addresses how principals and "mezzanine"-level leaders—those who serve as intermediaries between teachers and principals (teacher leaders, coaches, and those in similar roles)—work in concert to ensure effective conditions for teachers and students to learn and grow.

Chapter 5 provides a definition of and tools to create a shared understanding of high-quality instruction, also known as an instructional model. The chapter builds on the argument that a school district should have a cogent and coherent strategy for educational improvement that does not vary a great deal from school to school. It discusses why it is crucial that everyone in a district work with the same model for good instruction, what such a model should include, and how a shared understanding of high-quality instruction might be generated for the greatest benefit.

Part 3: Monitoring and Continuous Improvement (Chapters 6 and 7)

The final section of the book is dedicated to how, once your Disciplined Strategic Plan is in place, you can monitor and adjust implementation over time to facilitate continuous improvement and growth.

Chapter 6 begins with a discussion of accountability in the context of strategic planning and then highlights how to create data collection and assessment tools to help ensure the right information is collected to allow for effective decisions to be made regarding the plan's progress. The chapter closes with a discussion of why it is important to create routines that move us toward a state of constant growth and improvement and to weather the rapidly changing needs of our teachers and students in an ever-shifting environment.

Finally, Chapter 7 steps away from sharing the why, what, and how of the Disciplined Strategic Planning process to consider its potential impact over time.

Across all these sections, the reader will also hear stories from the fictionalized Ashburn district as their superintendent, Dr. Maria Jenkins, leads their strategic planning process. Ashburn will serve as an anchoring common experience as we present and support the use of various planning tools and protocols of disciplined strategic planning. In this way, our emphasis on exploring the Why (i.e., the principles) and the How (i.e., the processes) is what makes this book special and, we hope, useful to you and your teams as you engage in this critically important work.

Acknowledgments

We would like to thank our colleagues at the Connecticut Center for School Change and the University of Connecticut for all their help, advice, guidance, patience, generosity, and really excellent questions. We could not ask for better coworkers.

We also thank those people who blur the lines between family, friends, and colleagues, and whose support—intellectual and emotional—over many years has got us to where we are now: Rose Asera, Sarah Birkeland, Elaine Chin, Ken Foote, Ann O'Doherty, Fran Rabinowitz, Jim Silva, Carol Stevenson, Andrea Casteneda, Sarah Anderson, Mikii Bendotti, and Jeremiah Jordan. We would also like to thank our first teachers—our parents, Vicki and Ronald Weiner and Robert and Magdalene Stevenson—for doing such an incredible job.

We owe an enormous debt of gratitude to the hundreds of teachers, leaders, and coaches over the years who have been willing to engage with us in conversations about strategy, leadership, planning, and teaching. None of the ideas in this book would have been worth anything without being cocreated, field-tested, and, in some cases, debunked. As we like to say, thank you for the feedback.

Finally, we would like to thank all the educators who work tirelessly every day to ensure all our kids are getting what they need to thrive. You have always been essential and deserving of our collective praise and admiration and a system that values you, pays you fairly, and treats you as learners striving to enhance your practice. We hope this book is worthy of you, and that you will engage with us as you put some of the contents into practice.

Isobel Stevenson
Storrs, Connecticut
IStevenson@CTSchoolChange.org
@isobeltx

Jennie M. Weiner
Somerville, Massachusetts
Jennie.Weiner@UConn.edu
@jennieweiner

eResources

Keep an eye out for the eResources icon throughout this book, which indicates resources that are available online to be downloaded, printed, copied, and/or manipulated to suit your individualized use. You can access these downloads by visiting the book's page on the publisher's website under "Support Materials." Visit https://www.routledge.com/9780367331702.

Setting the Stage

Strategic Planning for Continuous Improvement

Welcome to the Strategy Playbook for Educational Leaders! We are thrilled to engage with you on this journey. The purpose of this book is to provide a better way to do strategic planning for continuous improvement and to offer concrete tools for participation in this process.

In our 50 or so combined years of work as coaches, researchers, district specialists, administrators, and teachers, we learned a lot about how schools and districts might think and plan more efficiently and effectively. We want to help you in your planning efforts by suggesting guiding principles and processes for developing plans that put more emphasis on the thinking behind the strategy and less on compliance. In other words, we want these plans and the process of creating them to work for you!

In this opening chapter, we introduce the big themes of the book and what makes our disciplined planning principles different from what you have likely experienced in the past. Specifically, you will see four big principles of disciplined planning that we will return to again and again:

- Equity
- Logic
- Capacity
- Coherence

These principles undergird our approach to planning and our subsequent recommended processes. These processes are introduced in Chapter 3, as is our tool to keep all your thinking organized: the **Disciplined Strategy Map**.

To aid in understanding these principles and processes, each chapter includes a case study drawn from our experiences of working with districts and schools as they endeavored to take an approach that went beyond tinkering or compliance to systemic redesign for continuous improvement.

In the following vignette, we introduce our main protagonist, Superintendent Maria Jenkins. She is not a real person, but she is modeled closely after strong superintendents we have worked with. She is well versed in the principles and processes we will explore in this book, and is about to engage in another year of planning using this knowledge. We will follow the story of her district's planning process throughout the book as a means of anchoring the process of Disciplined Strategic Planning. In future chapters, we will begin with Superintendent Jenkins' and her district's experiences to help anchor the conversation in practice.

Introducing Superintendent Jenkins

Superintendent Maria Jenkins sat down at her desk to start thinking about the design of a strategic plan for her district, Ashburn. She was in her first year as superintendent and wanted to get this right. While she knew this process would be time consuming and sometimes challenging, Maria was also aware that she was well positioned to engage in this work. Her board and community were behind her, the school administrators were a strong team, and she was pleased at the way things were going in Ashburn since her arrival.

From her experience in her previous district, Maria knew any changes she wanted to make would be much easier if she could justify them by saying she was responding to community and/or staff requests and/or concerns. She was therefore happy to spend her first few months listening and learning, as she was confident people who lived and worked in the district would have a great deal of insight into what was working and what should be improved. She also knew it was really important for the board to feel they were fully informed, consulted, and involved in her thinking, so when the chair of the board suggested it would be a good time for them to revisit the district's strategic plan, she was glad to do so.

Enrolling approximately 20,000 students and comprising nine elementary, four middle, and three high schools, Ashburn is a growing community. One of the state's poorest cities, Ashburn serves a diverse group of families across several demographic variables. This diversity is reflected in Ashburn's schools. While access and outcomes among different groups of students (Black, Latinx, English language learners, special education, etc.) remain an issue, differences in assessed areas are smaller than state averages. At the same time, there remains variability across schools in terms of their overall performance, school culture, and relationships with family and community.

Maria was responsible for creating strategic plans in the past, first as a principal and then as an associate superintendent in her prior district, and she found these plans less than helpful. Her experience with district and school improvement planning was that it was more about templates, "wordsmithing," and compliance, and did little to shape the daily work of administrators and teachers.

Maria knew she had to think about several things to start with, and there could be other considerations related to the planning process that hadn't occurred to her yet. She started making a list:

1. Need a process that includes all stakeholders but that isn't unwieldy and doesn't end up as a 70-page document that nobody ever looks at!

2. Need to focus on instruction—won't reach aspirations for students unless their experience in classrooms every day is a match for those goals.

3. Need a document that makes it easy to see how the work that we plan to do leads to improved outcomes for students—an infographic? Chart? Something that fits on one page but that is actually useful?

4. Find a way to connect the work and the plan without creating unnecessary bureaucracy/driven by compliance.

5. Capacity building has to be included, not a separate thing.

6. Need a plan to create the plan!

She decided to take this list to the administrative team and ask for their help to create a proposal to take to the board regarding what the process and the resulting document should look like.

Why This Book?

Long before the idea for this book was hatched, we independently spent many years in various roles supporting schools and districts in strategic planning: Isobel as a teacher leader, principal, central office administrator, coach, and consultant; Jennie as a coach, consultant, state turnaround specialist, and university professor. As a result, each of us concluded that even with well-intentioned people doing their best to make it work, planning as implemented in schools and school systems was, on the whole, a colossal waste of time.

Rather than an opportunity to reflect and strategize for the future, plans were often made at the last minute and in isolation from the real work of the school. There was no sense of continuity from one year's plan to the next, and these plans often lacked benchmarking tools or useful outcome measures to ensure appropriate movement of students *and* adults toward the goals. Interventions often appeared to be driven more by state and district mandates than by students' and teachers' needs.

People tasked with creating these plans also seemed highly stressed, often having been asked to produce a plan in a matter of days or without knowing the state or district's goals or the resources available to support their efforts. In the end, much of the activity became what Meyer and Rowan (1977) would call "myth and ritual": a grand show, more for the benefit of outsiders than to truly promote improvement. The plans then tended to sit on a shelf, brought out for accountability purposes and little else.

Does this sound familiar?

With such patterns repeating themselves as we worked in different places, we were frustrated. In addition to seeing hardworking people expend their most valuable resource—time—on an activity that seemed to bear little fruit, we both believed that strategic planning, when done right and in a disciplined way, can be really helpful. We wanted to help those engaged in planning feel less like Sisyphus and more like Odysseus (it's hard, but he makes it back!).

At the same time, neither of us had a strong sense of why folks were having such a hard time with planning, or specifically how to make it better. As a result, we both spent a lot of our collective careers trying to come up with solutions to this "planning problem" through trial and error.

Once we started working together, we came to the conclusion that the field was lacking two things:

- A guiding framework for understanding the purpose and principles of strategy.
- Concrete and clear processes for turning the principles of strategy into a plan that would make sense.

This, we felt, was why planning was not working.

We began searching for existing frameworks and tools to solve the problem as we now understood it. We found a lot of research on what schools should put in their plans to improve student learning and behavior (that is, interventions) and how to do things like write effective goals. But there was almost nothing on the guiding principles of strategic planning for continuous improvement in schools or how to go about it. No one was addressing the burning questions, such as: Why do it this way? How does this plan fit with larger improvement goals? How much goes in the plan? What comes first? Who needs to be part of the discussion? How do we appropriately measure our progress?

So, we created and tested our own ideas about what such guidance might look like. The result of these efforts is this book.

While we are excited to share our insights, we readily acknowledge that those most likely reading this book (district and school administrators and teacher leaders) may come to it quite frustrated at the current state of play. Such readers (that is, you) might be skeptical of yet another book to support planning and improvement. You might even be doubtful about planning itself, particularly given the continued accountability pressures and the multiple top-down policies that frequently dictate what schools implement year to year. We get it, and so throughout the book we do our best to be up-front about the continued challenges schools and districts face during this process even when planning improves.

There might also be some among you who don't care a lick about guiding frameworks and principles and are already asking, "When will they quit this yammering and just give me the tools to get it done?" If you fall into that camp, feel free to skip to Chapter 3, where we introduce the processes and provide our tool—the Disciplined Strategy Map—to get you started.

For everyone else, we hope you will stick around and learn a bit more about how a lack of principles or disciplined approach has made planning such a mess, and how we can change that.

How Planning Became a Compliance Exercise

Perhaps you remember what school improvement planning was like in the 1990s, when total quality management (TQM) and site-based decision-making were in vogue. As with many innovations, sometimes a lot is lost in translation between the idea and its implementation. In the case of TQM, the result was often a lot of focus on goals that were unrealistic or did not promote equity, and on interventions that tended to be more oriented toward compliance than continuous improvement.

First, there was a heavy emphasis on goals. Outcomes were supposed to be specific, measurable, attainable, realistic, and timely (SMART), and a lot of time was spent making sure this occurred. It was easy to get the impression that the goals themselves were what mattered—if you chose the right goal, you would be more likely to meet it. It was as if the goals themselves had the power to produce good outcomes, regardless of the resources available to enact them. As a result, those in schools and at the central office spent a lot of time perseverating over the goals and their semantics.

We have both sat in very long meetings in which teams spent hours coming up with the "right goal." For example, there were the many high school teams who struggled to agree on the right graduation goal. They asked, "Should we make the goal that 100% of incoming freshmen graduate in four years, even if we don't think it's realistic? Because if we don't, does that mean we are saying that we don't care about all kids? Plus the goal really *is* that 100% graduate. But if we do say 100% and we don't meet that goal, will we get in trouble? Should we say six years? How about five?"

When these are the questions, there are no right answers.

It often felt that it was important to choose BHAGs—big, hairy, and audacious goals—regardless of whether they were rooted in any real evidence or grounded in goals of equity and inclusion. The format of the Adequate Yearly Progress goals associated with No Child Left Behind was an example of this orientation. *Not* choosing BHAGs became an indicator that you weren't serious about improvement, or that you weren't willing to work hard enough to reach them. In the worst cases, it was thought that merely creating a BHAG was a predictor of reaching it.

The result of these struggles over goals was the continued piling on of consequences for underperforming schools, the demoralization of the educator workforce, and—important for our discussion—a sense that planning was inconsequential or even foolhardy. It turns out not to be true that an ambitious goal inevitably leads to an amazing result.

It was based on these often unrealistic and problematic goals that school improvement teams built their plans. Frequently presented as a list of tasks to be completed or a template to be filled out, these plans tended to be procedural in nature (first, second, third, etc.) and focused on things like when committees would meet to talk about the goal, who was going to do what, what training would be provided, and the date by which all this was going to be accomplished. Each goal had its own comprehensive list of action steps, with some plans growing unmanageably long. Isobel confesses to writing one as a principal that was more than 70 pages, and Jennie remembers reading a district plan that was over 270 pages!

To help streamline the process and hold schools accountable for creating and implementing their plans, districts and state departments of education often created elaborate templates for how they wanted school improvement plans written. In some cases, states even created standard templates required of all schools and districts. Often, these were well-intentioned attempts to minimize the number of documents that schools had to submit. For example, a school might no longer have to submit a separate Title I plan as there was a universal improvement plan that covered everything. Sometimes the templates, either district- or state-mandated, tried to force the school to follow a certain process to generate its plans. The template could include, for example, questions about what data were used to generate the plan, what the analysis of these data revealed, and how community stakeholders were engaged to decide on the appropriate goals.

And yet, despite encompassing many rules in what appeared to be an attempt to institutionalize data-based decision-making and create meaningful change, processes to create the plan, and the plans themselves infrequently included deep discussion about equity or changing practice—the primary process for producing results in schools. Moreover, these plans rarely created the impression that teachers were supposed to teach differently or reflect on how they thought about and understood their relationship to their students.

This is strange, when you think about it, as the organizational consultant who is frequently cited as the instigator of data-driven planning, W. Edwards Deming (1986), was all about process. His book *Out of the Crisis* is a kind of manifesto about how generations of business owners had not paid enough attention to the processes being used in generating their results. Some of his ideas were translated into familiar slogans: "If you do what you've always done, you'll get what you've always gotten," "The definition of madness is doing the same thing over and over and expecting a different result," and "Every system is perfectly designed to achieve the results it gets."

Perhaps it is the case that in your school or district you participate in an annual cycle of goal setting, filling out templates to create a plan, submission of the plan for feedback and approval, and working with committees, departments, or grade-level teams to implement the plan—all with the sinking feeling that none of it will amount to real change. Perhaps you're frustrated as the plan you created seems to have no life outside its place on the shelf. Perhaps you're looking for suggestions for how to give the process more meaning and traction.

In that case, you're in the right place, because that's exactly what we're going to do in this book.

In the next section, we define our four guiding principles of strategic planning: Equity, Logic, Capacity, and Coherence. Doing so provides an opportunity to help us understand what we argue is the real intent of strategic planning—to be able to articulate, monitor, and intervene in the learning process to ensure effective and equitable access, experience, and outcomes, including enhancements to teachers' professional culture, knowledge, and skills.

Guiding Principles of Disciplined Strategic Planning

As we mentioned, one of the reasons strategic planning went so wrong in education is the lack of a guiding framework to ground the work. In the absence of such a framework, the now-normalized twin concepts of accountability and performance outcomes drove the planning processes. The result was an emphasis on compliance, expediency, and what Day and Gu (2007) call "performativity" (a focus on easily generated indicators, such as standardized test scores and teacher evaluations), rather than organizational learning over time. Researchers have identified a variety of problems with such an approach, including making teaching less professional and narrowing the curriculum to tested subjects. To this list of problems, we'd add the deterioration of planning.

Here, we take a step to reclaim this narrative and put forward what we view as more appropriate and fruitful principles on which to base strategic planning. Derived through research and our own experiences, these principles often appear as critical attributes in both the continuous improvement literature and the planning literature.

Equity

We believe the driving or superordinate principle that should guide all planning processes is equity. Equity is grounded in the concept of fairness and when applied to education, as highlighted by the OECD, focuses on ensuring that students' social circumstances (e.g., gender, ethnicity, race, class, etc.) do not serve as obstacle to their achieving their academic potential and that all students receive the resources and supports necessary to reach that potential. It is critical that any plan should increase the likelihood that all students, and particularly those who have been historically minoritized and marginalized, have equitable access, opportunities, and outcomes. This requires the identification and elimination of the inequities (structural and otherwise) that contribute to disproportionate learning and achievement by students of certain groups, while ensuring that all students are prepared for a productive and meaningful life. It means that those in charge of school systems and working in schools (that is, white people) often need to learn about and understand systems of oppression and how we collectively participate in and uphold them. And yet, this focus and aligned activities still seem to be missing from plans and planning processes.

While many of the plans we have seen include mission statements and other documents that either explicitly name equity as an organizational value or, more often, imply equity by using the term "all students," we also know

11

that many schools and districts have been unable to make meaningful progress in raising the attainment of their lowest-achieving students or closing gaps between students of different racial and/or ethnic backgrounds on a variety of important outcomes (performance, graduation rates, attendance, etc.).

Discriminatory disciplinary practices, resource allocations that favor schools with fewer students from minoritized groups, and curricula that fail to recognize the diverse cultural backgrounds and contributions of students and their communities are common in our schools and must be addressed as part of any strategy for improvement. Whiteness is still often treated as "neutral," with little action taken on the part of educators in predominately white-serving schools to critically examine it and the ways in which it operates in society. (This bias applies to other societal structures as well, such as patriarchy, heteronormativity, etc.). White educators often do not have the opportunity to engage meaningfully in understanding white bias and other forms of oppression and how they often unknowingly support these destructive systems. There are no equity-neutral policies—or, as Ibram X. Kendi (2019) has highlighted, there are only racist and antiracist policies (and this concept can be applied to other forms of discrimination as well).

However, rather than tackle some of these more systemic issues in their plans, schools tend to focus solely on raising expectations for students of color, students from poverty, and students with special needs. Schools are generally ill-equipped to put in place practices to change the experience of these students in such a way that their learning improves and to enact an antiracist or liberation-oriented approach to education. We can do better.

Logic

Our thinking about logic is grounded in the construct of the logic model, which is a tool researchers and program evaluators have been using for a long time to measure the effectiveness of a treatment, program, or intervention. A logic model seeks to make transparent the relationship between a strategy and its ultimate outcome to determine if the actions performed in service of the strategy accomplish what they were intended to accomplish. It does that by creating a flow chart showing connections along the path and identifying and measuring indicators along the way of how intent and impact are actually unfolding.

Logic modeling, and what we call "strategy mapping," is characterized by four components:

- resources (inputs)
- activities (aspects of implementation)
- outputs (observable products of the activities that are part of the chain leading to the intended outcomes)
- outcomes (the results of the activities)

These components are put together graphically to reveal their relationships and thus provide opportunities to better understand how one element impacts the other and the intended outcomes (Lawton et al., 2014). Any strategy, and any strategic plan, should clearly and logically articulate the theory of action, or the anticipated chain of causation, underlying the selected interventions.

Essential to this process is the need to clarify what both the adults and the students at all levels of the system will need to know and do as a result of the introduction of an intervention or plan. For example, rather than simply saying that in response to student needs in math, a new curriculum will be implemented and thus student achievement will increase (the magical thinking or "here a miracle occurs" approach to change), a strategy with a focus on process would highlight the need to train teachers in the new curriculum. It would also focus on building their sense of the substance of the curriculum; it would treat teachers as learners who need support to shift their beliefs and actions.

Such an approach would help make sure everyone was clear on the following points:

- How will the strategy and associated intervention challenge current practices and better connect to students' experiences and needs (equity)?
- What is the purpose of the strategy and interventions and their relationship to other initiatives, structures, and policies in the district and the building (coherence)?
- How will implementation be supported and monitored over time (capacity)? (See Figure 1.1)

Initiative Audit

There are several possible purposes of an initiative audit:

To list all the initiatives currently underway in an organization (to the best of knowledge of those participating!) so that:

1. Participants may discover whether everyone has the same knowledge of all the initiatives/programs currently being implemented in the school/district;
2. Participants may discover whether everyone has the same understanding of the school or district's strategy for improvement;
3. Leaders may assess whether the programs being implemented represent a focus on a small number of high-leverage initiatives;
4. Leaders may have data to use as a basis for prioritization.

We find that the closer educators are to the classroom, the less clear they are regarding their district's priorities for improvement—in other words, teachers tend to be less clear than principals and superintendents, even though the teachers are the ones who are often implicated in the implementation. Therefore, in order to make the best use of the initiative audit, it is really important to:

a) Include employees at several levels of the organization, including but not limited to community members, paraeducators, teachers, students, principals, and the superintendent;
b) Give everyone the chance to write down their own thoughts and ideas before sharing;
c) Make it more likely that everyone will share by ensuring that the people with the most power share last;
d) Not betray dismay or confusion when participants make contributions to the audit that you think are wrong, or let participants see that you are unhappy with the results of the audit.

Here are the steps for conducting the initiative audit:

1. Individually, take a few minutes to write down all the initiatives currently being operationalized in your school/district. Write each one on a separate Post-It note.

2. When you have captured them all, share with the other members of your team and make sure that you have one Post-It for each initiative.

3. Take all the Post-Its and group them by theme on a piece of chart paper.

Here are the steps for debriefing. These questions are a guide, and may vary depending on the reasons why the group is doing the audit:

1. What did you learn from doing this? For example:

   a. Did everyone on the team know about all the initiatives?

   b. Was it clear from the final grouping what the district is focused on?

   c. Are you working on too much? Too little? Just right?

2. What does this suggest to you about the problems you need to correct? These could include lack of clarity, lack of focus, or something else.

3. Given your answer to #2, what should be the focus of improvement for your district? For example, if lack of clarity is a problem, how are you going to address that?

Figure 1.1 Initiative Audit

It is this change to teacher knowledge and practice coupled with the new content and delivery to students (the instructional core) that will produce enhanced student achievement. Moreover, by unpacking the "how" or the temporal process of improvement and producing a hypothesized causal chain, individuals are empowered to collect data across the implementation trajectory and intervene when needed to enhance performance.

Capacity

While we are always enthusiastic to read plans with new and ambitious interventions, when we do so we often wonder about whether the districts and schools have the necessary resources (capacity) to pull them off. Though it is never fun to be the Debbie Downer ("Why can't we just try this innovative thing?"), she often gets a bad rap. More Debbies might also mean fewer under-capacity efforts with associated lackluster results. When we say capacity, we think of it as "the wherewithal to actually implement [a decision/intervention]. The capacity to use reform is the extent to which the [school] has the knowledge, skills, personnel, and other resources necessary to carry out decisions" (Firestone, 1989, p. 157). Though not explicitly stated here, this includes district infrastructure more broadly (policies, reporting structures, supports, etc.). In other words, a lot of things need to be in place to ensure an intervention will be successful, and these things may not be immediately available, or even possible to get.

Also embedded in this concept of capacity is the degree to which districts and schools have the structures, culture, and time, and the human, financial, and physical resources (that is, the infrastructure) to enable those on the ground to make each and every element of the intervention work. For example, one intervention we often see being proposed in plans is data teams. Often these plans also include money for data coaches and sometimes changes to the school schedule to facilitate meeting times. While these additional resources would undoubtedly be helpful, it might also be necessary to consider the current assessment practices in the school and whether the district has the technical know-how and equipment to process different forms of data quickly and efficiently and to distribute it to teachers in a usable format. If not, it is difficult to see how the data teams can effectively engage in their work or produce positive outcomes. In such a scenario, the district and the school would need to plan for building capacity in these areas if they want the teams to be successful. With this example in mind, we consider capacity and the work of capacity building to be an essential principle of effective planning.

Coherence

Our fourth planning principle is coherence. Coherence is the degree of connectivity and alignment within and across a system as well as its alignment with existing infrastructure and resources in the system (Elmore et al., 2014). Coherence enhances the likelihood a plan will be successful (Trujillo, 2013) and suggests that those developing the plan need to pay attention to:

- The degree selected interventions match the identified needs.
- Whether parts of the system work together to make these interventions possible (resource alignment, structure and policy alignment, etc.).
- Whether there were signs of connectivity over time—both across and within years.

While it might seem obvious that we should create plans that are grounded in need, feasible, and build over time, such coherence is relatively rare. It's worth mentioning that the more there is in a plan, the harder it is to keep the plan coherent. Focusing on coherence has implications regarding the number of interventions that can be successfully implemented at any one time (only a few interventions at a time!).

We acknowledge schools and districts are often pushed to adopt numerous interventions regardless of their specific alignment to stated needs due to funding, accountability pressures, etc. This, of course, makes building coherence more difficult. We would argue that, if forced into such a position, it is still important for those creating the plans to create coherence around the interventions to help ensure the other principles are in place. If not, it is unlikely the mandated interventions (or others) will get the traction they deserve and need.

A Return to Principles

We will return to these four principles at the end of each chapter to help draw connections between them and the processes we advocate. For now, however, let's move on to explore the concepts of strategy and continuous improvement and how they serve to drive the planning process.

References

Day, C., & Gu, Q. (2007). Variations in the conditions for teachers' professional learning and development: Sustaining commitment and effectiveness over a career. *Oxford Review of Education, 33*(4), 423–443.

Deming, W. Edwards (1986). *Out of the crisis.* Cambridge, MA: Massachusetts Institute of Technology Center for Advanced Engineering Study.

Elmore, R. F., Forman, M. L., Stosich, E. L., & Bocala, C. (2014). *The internal coherence assessment protocol & developmental framework: Building the organizational capacity for instructional improvement in schools.* Cambridge, MA: Harvard University.

Firestone, W. A. (1989). Using reform: Conceptualizing district initiative. *Educational Evaluation and Policy Analysis, 11*(2), 151–164.

Kendi, I. X. (2019). *How to be an antiracist.* First Edition. New York, NY: One World.

Lawton, B., Brandon, P. R., Cicchinelli, L., & Kekahio, W. (2014). Logic models: A tool for designing and monitoring program evaluations. REL 2014–007. *Regional Educational Laboratory Pacific.*

Meyer, J. W., & Rowan, B. (1977). Institutionalized organizations: Formal structure as myth and ceremony. *American Journal of Sociology, 83*(2), 340–363.

Trujillo, T. (2013). The reincarnation of the effective schools research: Rethinking the literature on district effectiveness. *Journal of Educational Administration, 51*(4), 426–452.

What Is Strategy?

Vignette: Understanding Strategy

Having set to creating the district's new strategic plan, Maria devoted time at the next several administrative team meetings to talk about strategy and improvement planning. Specifically, providing them a tool on how to engage, she asked the principals and their teams to prepare an inventory of current programming and interventions as a prelude to talking about their effectiveness. Discussing their findings together and hearing the administrators generate a list of programs that included some she had never heard of, she realized that the district was initiative heavy and strategy poor.

There was a clear need to engage more deeply about equity in the district. Principals seemed to take for granted that because gaps in achievement were smaller than in surrounding districts, they were "good enough." There also seemed to be a lack of understanding of how current policies and programs might be creating other, equally problematic disproportionate outcomes for students. For example, enrollment in honors and AP classes throughout the district was predominately white and middle class. People seemed to accept this as the norm rather than consider how entry into these classes was often contingent on teacher recommendation—a practice that is often shown to produce biased results.

She also realized there was need among her principals and district staff to better understand the nature of strategy and how it was different from planning. Only the week before, she'd had a challenging conversation with one of her principals regarding the planning process. She called him to talk about the need for the new planning. His response was a litany of resources and programs other districts were implementing that he thought they should be using too. To justify these requests, the principal talked about the continuing performance gaps in the district. However, when Maria pressed him on how these programs would directly address current needs and asked for data about the effectiveness of current programs aimed at enhancing this same goal, he was unable to provide answers.

To help all her administrators—whether district- or school-based—rethink strategy and how to approach improvement, Maria began to look for examples of strategies in newspaper and magazine articles. She found several: China and its strategy for increasing the markets for its products by investing in infrastructure in poorer countries; Enron and its strategy of manipulation and deception to capture energy markets; the strategy of the leaders of the civil rights movement to claim the moral high ground and lean on its army of volunteers.

Maria explained that she really wanted a document to be created that would set direction for the district in the form of a vision, a mission, and goals, but that would also:

1. Communicate the district's commitment to equitable access, experiences, and outcomes for all students, and the plan to actually attain those opportunities and outcomes.
2. Be clear and logical: show how the action of the superintendent would lead to work by leaders and teachers that would lead to improved outcomes for all students.
3. Include capacity building for leaders and teachers as an essential component, not an afterthought.
4. Make it clear the district was aligned in working toward meeting the needs of students.

As a team, they began to think about what the development process could look like, and who should be involved in creating the plan once they had the process figured out.

Chapter Overview

In this chapter, we talk about the intellectual core of the planning process: strategy. After studying many district and school documents over the years that were titled "strategic plan," we rarely saw a true strategy driving the proposed actions—in Mintzberg's (1987) language, there was a plan but no ploy. Instead, many plans seemed oriented more toward fulfilling requirements for creating goals and action steps and less toward designing an approach to realize their aspirations. This chapter, then, is about strategy and how we might conceptualize it and use it for planning. (For those who want to get into action, you're welcome to skip ahead to Chapters 3 and 4, where we get into the nitty-gritty of planning and creating a plan.)

Defining Disciplined Strategy

In our conversations about this book, we found ourselves disagreeing about the best way to define strategy. Is it a framework? No, too technical! A set of guidelines to reach a goal? No, that sounds like a diet! Finally, we agreed that part of the problem was that we were conflating a *strategy* with *strategy*. We understand that this sounds pedantic, but we are trying to make an important point: engaging in strategic work is both a process and an outcome. There is the means, which is engaging in the heavy cognitive labor of thinking through all the aspects of the work that the organization needs to do to fulfill its mission, and there is the end, which is having an understanding of what the work to accomplish the outcome entails.

Through our conversations, we also realized that the assumptions and values underlying a strategy need to be considered, because how outcomes are achieved is just as important as achieving them. If, for example, all that matters in your plan is that student scores go up on a literacy test, then it's hard for teachers and leaders to resist the temptation to narrow the curriculum to focus on improving scores, perhaps giving up instruction in the arts or forgoing reading literature in favor of completion of worksheets that are aligned to the content and format of the test.

In this way, every educational decision is a referendum on the principles of your organization; it reflects your beliefs about what really matters. Not all strategies are equal, but figuring out what makes one strategy better than another is often difficult. We want to help, and therefore we offer our driving principles of Equity, Logic, Coherence, and Capacity to create some guideposts to help discern whether a strategy is "good" across multiple parameters. We name this approach Disciplined Strategy, and when we get to planning, Disciplined Strategic Planning.

A strategic plan is the physical manifestation of the understanding that has been reached of what needs to happen for the organization to meet its goals. Ideally, then, a plan, a strategy, and a strategic plan would all mean the same thing, because strategy and plan are two sides of the same coin. Strategy without a plan is just a dream, and a plan without strategy is pointless.

What does this mean in terms of definitions of these terms? *Strategy* is an informed and intentional set of aligned choices about actions to generate a desired outcome. To be effective, it must become a *strategy*: a plan that describes the work to be done (i.e., aspiration), accounts for capacity (i.e., identifies current and needed resources), stipulates leadership action (i.e., includes a theory of action[1] outlining the organization's beliefs about what will lead to success), addresses any other challenges that need to be met to generate the outcome, and includes opportunities to collect important data along the way to improve the strategy.

To put our definition of a strategy into the context of schools and districts, we might imagine an aspiration could be to enhance equity throughout the district. As Maria chose to do in the Chapter 1 vignette, we might suggest that the district undertake an equity audit (Skrla et al., 2009).

The next step would be for those in the district to identify how change happens relative to enhancing equity. It might be that they think improving teachers' knowledge and skills relative to equity and social justice-oriented practices will enhance all students' experiences. These enhanced experiences would serve to increase opportunity and outcomes for students who have been traditionally marginalized. The strategy then might be to shift professional development to focus on antiracist practices and curriculum while reforming the current discipline structures and systems.

Looking around the district, we would then broadly identify current and future capacity to make this goal a reality. For example, there might be pockets of teachers with training in restorative practices, access to university supports in social justice leadership, curricular supports focus on culturally sustaining pedagogy, instructional coaches, community resources, etc.

Components of the District Strategy

Vision	To enhance equity in opportunity and outcome throughout the district.
Capacity	Teacher expertise in restorative practices; university intellectual supports; access to high-quality, culturally sustaining curriculum.
Theory of Action	If we enhance teachers' knowledge and skills regarding equity and socially just practices, students will have greater access to the instructional core and better outcomes.
Strategy	We will shift our resources toward antiracist practices and invest in restorative discipline practices, thereby increasing teachers' and administrators' capacity to engage with students in ways that are equitable and produce more equitable outcomes.

While this may all seem relatively straightforward, choosing a strategy that is effective and will support getting you to your desired destination (and not somewhere else) can be quite difficult because while there are many ways to achieve a narrow outcome, it is not always possible to know what trade-offs may occur as a result of putting effort toward or betting on a particular strategy. But to repeat our earlier point, while there are lots of strategies, not all are created equal. To help mitigate the likelihood of selecting a less effective strategy (that is, one with more negative impacts or trade-offs), we suggest the use of our guiding principles.

 Equity

First, it is essential that equity guides any strategy. A good strategy is one that helps to bridge gaps and ensures more opportunities and access for previously minoritized and/or underserved individuals, groups, programs, etc. To help support this orientation, as you consider or weigh different strategies, it would be useful to ask questions about who might gain or lose from using resources in this way. Who is included in the strategy? Why? Who is excluded? Why? It might also be useful to unpack some of the assumptions guiding the strategy. For example, does the approach assume that traditional power relationships are best left intact (principals bringing ideas to teachers, teachers "inviting" families in, students receiving instruction, etc.)? Why? What other mechanisms might be available? Such questions are important because as a strategy prioritizes a particular approach, it also deprioritizes others.

For instance, a new strategy could lead a district to move resources, such as counselors or paraprofessionals, away from certain types of tasks to others. If paraprofessionals move from primarily serving the needs of special education students who are mainstreamed, what will happen when they are retrained to support small-group math instruction? Is this an equitable solution to enhance math? What are the trade-offs? Who benefits?

Given that trade-offs are inevitable in developing a strategy, it's important to take a step back and add the following caveats:

- Additional resources won't solve the problem (though they could help), nor will the admonition to "do more with less" (which never helps). Choices require trade-offs and trade-offs cannot be made to go away, only mitigated.

- Too often, priorities tend to reflect the values and interests of dominant or more powerful groups with a higher level of willingness to cut or ignore the priorities of minoritized or marginalized groups. Given the already disparate demographics between the mostly white middle-class school and district leaders and teachers (those often in charge of strategic planning) and the increasingly more racially and ethnically diverse and financially needy students and families schools serve, we need to be very careful in the development of strategy. Specifically, we need to make sure privilege doesn't drive decision-making in our schools and districts as we work toward improvement.

Logic

Logic, particularly as it is applied to strategy, is the notion that all the work the strategy calls for must have a clear and causal relationship with the desired result. This can be problematic in school systems where the focus has long been solely on outcomes and not the processes (e.g., teaching and learning practices) that facilitate these outcomes.

It is also the case that many of the key decisions and actions those at the district office take are several degrees separated from the classroom. The superintendent makes leadership moves that depend on principals who make leadership moves that depend on teacher leaders and coaches to prepare teachers to enact certain practices in the classrooms. In other words, change is multifaceted and complex and, we believe, can easily get away from you if you do not have a guiding framework to keep track of each piece and its relationship to all the other things you are doing.

A strategy map is important because it makes explicit and clear how these many moving parts connect with and impact one another in service of your goal (i.e., the chain of causation). Anyone should be able to look at the strategy and say, "Ah yes, I see why the superintendent is charged with doing that. It's because the principals will be able to do this with the department chairs, so that the department chairs will do this with the teachers, so that the teachers will do this with their students." In other words, an interested reader of the strategy should be able to chart the through-line of the plot.

The logic driving the strategy is only as good as its underlying premise or theory of action. The theory of action as a component of the strategy is a manifestation of the organization's beliefs about what will lead to success as the organization defines it. Let's take as an example a plan based on a reading program. The theory of action would be something like, "If all students receive 90 minutes of instruction a day in X reading program, then student achievement in reading will increase."

Logic dictates, then, that the strategy designers answer the question "What do teachers need to learn to teach X reading program the way that it ought to be taught?" And then the next question would be "What work do coaches need to do with teachers so that teachers learn those things?," followed by "What do coaches need to learn so that they can support teachers the way we need them to?" And then the strategy designers would ask the same questions about principals, and so on.

It's important to point out that while it's possible to build a perfectly good chain of causation on a faulty theory of action and a nice-sounding strategy, a well-constructed logic model will point this out. For example, over the years we have seen districts use the construct of "learning styles" as a key driver of their interventions in their strategic plans. In these plans, the districts clearly articulate how this approach will enhance outcomes for both students and teachers. However, based on substantial research, we know that identifying and teaching to students' learning styles does not improve achievement. Therefore, while nicely written and well-articulated, these plans are unlikely to create the desired outcomes. In contrast, if the district had built a strong logic model, they would have been forced to include clear references regarding how they would monitor each part of the theory of action toward successfully implementing their strategy. As a result, the lack of effectiveness of this approach would become apparent early on in implementation, and the intervention or the larger plan would need to be adjusted to support effective implementation. In this way, a logic model can help you from going too far with a faulty theory, no matter how good it sounds.

Capacity

The work that the district strategy requires of educators depends on their possessing the capacity to do it. For example, a strategy anchored by teachers' employment of formative assessment and students' receiving better and more frequent feedback relies on teachers and administrators having a deep understanding of what distinguishes formative and summative assessment, how to employ formative assessment practices as a regular part of instruction, how to alter instruction as a result of formatively assessing students, what makes feedback effective in addition to being personalized and timely, and so on.

Often, we see plans that assume everyone already knows what they need to know to do what the plan involves. They contain few, if any, references to building capacity. The notion seems to be that enacting a plan is just like flipping a switch to the "on" position—everyone does what they are supposed to do when the plan tells them to do it. We know this is unlikely to occur—a fact many senior leaders acknowledge when probed about their plans. But because the format of their plan does not typically include a place for capacity building, they appear not to have considered it. Perhaps more importantly, funding is often linked to these plans and, as a result, the failure to mention these capacity-building components ensures they go unfunded.

In other cases, the plan contains only a cursory nod to capacity. A workshop is listed as an item in the action steps even though when we ask senior leaders about this, they do not really believe that a workshop on an instructional practice is sufficient to change classroom instruction. Or the plan says that there will be a plan for professional development—which is particularly baffling, as often the timeline for the development of such a plan is the middle of the fall semester.

Above all, capacity building is not a one-and-done event. Capacity to enact part of a strategy should never be dependent on a workshop, presentation, or conference. The most important aspect of capacity building is that it is long term, ongoing, and continuous: in other words, it should be accomplished through routines that are enacted throughout the district all the time. Instructional or leadership coaching, done properly, is a powerful routine. Action research—the study of one's own practice—is a powerful routine. Data teams and other collaborative arrangements among teachers and/or leaders are powerful when they are focused on building the capacity of the participants by engaging them in a cycle of continuous improvement: choosing a part of the strategy that is most likely to move the team closer to its goal, trying it out, collecting data, and using that data to learn and improve.

Almost never in the plans we have seen is there reference to capacity building beyond the role of teacher. But we know, from repeated experience, that holding a credential does not equip you with the skills you will need to support a strategy in a particular school or district. Context matters. We advocate that just as much attention should be paid to building leadership capacity as to instructional capacity.

While we press you to think about capacity in your schools and district, it is unnecessary to look far afield to do so. You can, and perhaps should, look to the people who are already doing what you value with the resources already available. In other words, find the "bright spots" (Heath & Heath, 2010) and "positive deviants" (Spreitzer & Sonenshein, 2004), then look to expand that capacity across the system.

How hard and time consuming the capacity building for a strategy will be depends on many factors. It might be relatively easy to implement a new program to engage students differently in the classroom around reading if the teachers are already strong in reading pedagogy, but it might be quite hard to prepare all the teachers on how to use technology in meaningful ways to enhance pedagogy. Every decision about strategy also entails a cost–benefit analysis involving expansion of capacity. A district will have to consider whether a better course of action (and a better use of resources) might be to build strategy around already-existing capacity.

Capacity building is more time consuming than plan designers realize. Sometimes this is because unforeseen events get in the way (we write this while schools are closed because of the COVID-19 crisis), but often it is because leaders underestimate, by quite a large margin, how much time it takes for teachers to feel comfortable shifting their practice to a new and different way of teaching. Remember, too, effective change comes not from doing lots and lots of things without the necessary resources and only sort of well. Instead, to make real and lasting change it's important to go deep and create interlocking systems in which all parts of the organization are well supported so they can work together to achieve one focused goal.

As we move on to discuss coherence, it's worth pointing out that if you're realistic about the amount of capacity you need to build and the resources it will take to build it, this will act as a constraint on your planning that will serve you well in ensuring your strategy is more coherent. In other words, capacity building may slow you down and/or make you prioritize where you place your energy and resources; if so, your strategy may be more coherent in the long run.

Coherence

We think of coherence, our fourth principle, as the extent to which the various parts of an organization are connected and aligned to facilitate the work of the district in reaching its vision. We know this is important from our own experience, but also because of research that shows districts with more coherence are more likely to produce gains in student achievement (Trujillo, 2013). To make decisions that help build coherence and move you closer to your goals, it's important to take time to consider what parts of your current work and the resources (e.g., human, financial, time), systems, and structures that undergird it matter most to achieve your goals. (See Chapter 4 on leadership for more information about these processes.)

Coherence has become something of a buzzword lately, and, as a result, district leaders are more aware than before of their responsibility to ensure that all parts of the organization—budget and operations, talent management, accountability, and so on—are aligned to the district mission.

However, we believe the component of district responsibility that would most benefit from tighter alignment across the system is instruction. This claim is bolstered by Johnson et al. (2015) and the conceptualization of coherence as the dynamic negotiation of school and district goals and external pressures to facilitate a tighter focus on teaching, learning, and improvement.

In most districts, the definition of good instruction is the district's teacher evaluation document. However, because one of its functions is to hold teachers accountable to a minimum standard for instruction, the descriptions of what is acceptable performance are necessarily broad. For the purposes of developing a powerful strategy, it's in the district's interest to generate a tight, cogent, narrowly focused definition of good instruction, for two major reasons.

First, the district should adopt a strategy that has the greatest chance of improving outcomes for students, and not all instructional practices are created equal when it comes to student learning. Rather than let individual schools or individual teachers choose how to teach, the district should promote a pedagogy aligned with its goals for students.

And second, because it's a great deal easier to support a narrowly defined vision for high-quality instruction than all practices that fall under the umbrella of the district's teacher evaluation plan, it's much more likely that the district will be able to change instructional practice when the resources of the district can be devoted to implementing a small set of mutually reinforcing teaching practices. For this reason, we devote Chapter 5 to high-quality instruction.

Of course, coherence in and of itself is not enough to ensure, or even contribute to, student success. Just as we make the point that a strategy is pointless if the underlying theory of action is weak, coherence is wasted if the organization is not aligned with an equity-focused and otherwise worthy vision. Coherence as a force for organizational improvement exists in service of a larger goal, not as an end itself. For some reason, in all the talk about coherence, that message does not always come through.

Another common issue we come across relating to coherence is that the district communicates new programs and plans but does not communicate what it is no longer doing. Educators in the organization don't know whether their leaders assume that those things are still being done, whether they're no longer wanting them done, or something else. So not only must the organization know both how to proceed and what to stop (or, as Michael Porter [1996, p.70] said, "the essence of strategy is choosing what not to do"), but it must also make clear what it means if an item from one year's plan is not carried over to the next.

Ask yourself and your team not only "What should we be doing (to reach our goal)?," but also "What shouldn't we be doing?" Indeed, we believe one of the most important features of a strong strategy is the identification and trimming of activities and infrastructure not aligned with the goal. Schools and districts are infamous for piling one program and structure upon another without getting rid of anything underneath. A good strategy should force people to name these issues and to create leverage for leaders to trim or add when needed.

Our examination of improvement plans has taught us that, within the time span of a given plan, there is generally alignment between the stated needs, goals, and interventions. In other words, there has clearly been thought given to what actions will lead to the achievement of goals. However, the connection between one year's plan and the next year's plan are generally very loose. What schools and districts decide to do in any given year is not a strong predictor of what they did the year before, or what they will do the following year.

This leads us to propose that coherence should not just be thought of as what is happening at a point in time, but should also be considered *through* time, because otherwise the experience of the people in the organization is choppy and sometimes confusing. No matter how well aligned the budget is to the district priorities or the professional development plan to the student outcomes, it will be impossible to convince teachers who cannot predict from one year to the next what the district's focus is that they are working in a coherent system.

Note

1 We use Argyris and Schön's (1974) construct of a theory of action to define it here as a testable proposition about the causal relationship between a set of actions that will produce a desired result. In so doing, we note that, in our experience, this definition does not often match reality. Instead, theories of action are left untested and used in lieu of, rather than as a component of, a strategy. The result is that, like many strategic plans, theories of action include lots of well-turned phrases but produce less meaningful changes to schools and school systems. We therefore de-emphasize this term, opting instead to focus on our principles to make the case for the need to create meaningful hypotheses regarding learning and change that can be, and are, regularly tested and modified (via changes to the interventions) to produce continuous improvement.

References

Argyris, C., & Schön, D. A. (1974). *Theory in practice: Increasing professional effectiveness.* San Francisco, CA: Jossey-Bass.

Heath, C., & Heath, D. (2010). *Switch: How to change when change is hard.* London, UK: Random House.

Johnson, S. M., Marietta, G., Higgins, M. C., Mapp, K. L. & Grossman, A. (2015). *Achieving coherence in district improvement: Managing the relationship between the central office and schools.* Cambridge, MA: Hearvard Education Press.

Mintzberg, H. (1987). The strategy concept: Five Ps for strategy. *California Management Review, 30*(1), 11–24.

Porter, M. E. (1996). What is strategy? *Harvard Business Review, 74*(6): 61–78.

Skrla, L., McKenzie, K. B., & Scheurich, J. J. (Eds.). (2009). *Using equity audits to create equitable and excellent schools.* Thousand Oaks, CA: Corwin Press.

Spreitzer, G. M., & Sonenshein, S. (2004). Toward the construct definition of positive deviance. *American Behavioral Scientist, 47*(6), 828–847.

Trujillo, T. (2013). The reincarnation of the effective schools research: Rethinking the literature on district effectiveness. *Journal of Educational Administration, 51*(4), 426–452.

Getting to Business

3

Building a Strategy

Vignette: Beginning the Planning Process

Tasked by her school board with revisiting the district's vision and mission, and based on her assessment that many internal stakeholders didn't know how the district was intending to improve outcomes, Maria needed a plan to develop the district strategy.

She knew several superintendents who had recently embarked on major community-involved processes. In at least two cases, the work was about creating a "portrait of the graduate" (Battelle for Kids, 2018) in response to reform efforts or accreditation requirements. In a nearby district, the superintendent had commissioned a far-reaching and comprehensive equity audit. He believed having qualitative and quantitative data everyone could access would help generate support for plans to address the issues. Maria and her team did some research and came up with an approach to create a strategic plan for the district that would involve revising the district vision, mission, and goals, and writing a set of plans based on a clearly articulated strategy for reaching their portrait of the graduate.

Maria recommended going through the process of developing the portrait of the graduate for Ashburn because she had been impressed by the work of other districts that had created sets of characteristics and competencies they wanted all students to acquire. These sets were then used to build the larger vision, mission, goals, and theory of action for the district in alignment with the portrait of the graduate. This made more sense to her than the vaguer statements she was familiar with that often passed as district vision documents.

Once the portrait of the graduate was developed, Ashburn's mission would be to pursue it, grounded in the district's values of fairness, kindness, and respect.

They would work on developing a strategy so the district could meet its ambitious goals for its graduates. She knew that coming up with a really inspiring and powerful model for what instruction needed to look like was going to be crucial.

In terms of identifying all the work that needed to be done to fulfill these aspirations, Maria took the suggestions generated by her administrative team and created several groups that she wanted to involve in the planning processes over the course of a month or so.

She also found a protocol from the Connecticut Center for School Change (see Figure 3.1) to follow for meeting with each group. This looked very different from the way she had experienced the creation of strategic plans in the past, with a PowerPoint explaining the process and a series of templates or worksheets to be filled out. She decided that most of the "juice" was in the conversations, so she asked participants to form small groups and focus on a series of guiding questions, capturing their responses and thinking on chart paper along the way.

She was excited and nervous to start and hoped that this time the plan would feel more authentic and connected to the everyday work of educators throughout the district.

Chapter Overview

In this chapter we describe our approach to creating strategy. The previous chapter laid out the principles that drive the creation of strategy: Equity, Logic, Capacity, and Coherence. This chapter describes in more practical terms the work necessary to create a strategy, along with tools you can use during the process. The first steps are to create a vision, a mission, and goals. Then you can begin the process of backward mapping to support the articulation of your plan and your theory of action.

Our experience is that schools and districts create visions, missions, and goals because they are required to and not because these activities ensure or promote change. We ask you to think about how vision, mission, and goals can be used to advance the work of improving student learning.

Next, we'll talk about the process of backward mapping (a process many of those in schools are familiar with already) and how it can be used to support the development of your plan and the theory of action within it. We'll show how such mapping might be incorporated into your plan and the associated Disciplined Strategy Map.

Before we go any further, we want to emphasize, again, that the purpose of any tools, protocols, and plans is to document thinking; they are not the ends in themselves. When designing any kind of plan or process, it's all too easy to slip into the trap of replacing one compliance activity with another. We'll give you a scenario of what this might look like.

Let's say that you're a superintendent and you're excited about the concept of strategy mapping. You want all the schools in your district to produce one. You're certain it will help them be more focused on continuous improvement. So, you make everyone read this book and you distribute multiple copies of the strategy mapping tool for principals to use as a template.

But the schools don't really understand the reasoning behind this change in the required template. Even if they did, they don't have the capacity or resources to meaningfully use the template as an engine of change. Or perhaps they consider the map to be a mandate, and so the principals sit by themselves in their offices and fill it out, without involving any stakeholders or gaining any buy-in. In these cases, the new template ends up being just as *pro forma* as the previous way of doing business. The key to avoiding such an unfortunate end is to remember that these tools are to be used in the context of the four principles. This will help keep your strategy on track for real change.

Backward Mapping

Before we start discussing visions, missions, and goals, we want to talk about a process for developing these elements: backward mapping. As described by Wiggins and McTighe (2005), when educators engage in a backward design approach to curriculum, they start with developing a very clear idea of the desired outcomes for all students and then figure out the work that needs to be done to make those outcomes a reality. Such an approach facilitates opportunities to carefully consider the current and needed resources, structures, and even classroom and school culture to ensure the goal will be reached.

Strategy Map

Goal/Area of Focus:			Theory of Action:
A. Central Office will	B. Principals will learn how to	C. Principals will	D. Instructional coaches will learn how to

Figure 3.1 Blank Strategy Map

Backward design, in the sense we're describing it, is a way to move from the vision, mission, and goals to the map. Specifically, it can help you discover how to create the necessary conditions for educators to facilitate the desired outcomes for students. The form we use in our work is very simple (Figure 3.1).

As you can see, the last column focuses on the vision—the end game—in this case, what you want students to know and be able to do as a result of

E. Instructional coaches will	F. Teachers will learn how to	G. Teachers will	H. Students will know and be able to

Figure 3.1 (Continued)

attending your schools. The top row of the map focuses on the mission, the goals, and the theory of action driving your work. Together, these articulate the strategy and are the areas of the map we will be focusing on in this chapter. In Chapter 4, we work to fill in first the left-hand columns (those focusing on leadership and creating conditions for continuous improvement); then, in Chapter 5, those on the right (those focused on the engine of improvement—instruction); and finally, in Chapter 6, the bottom of the map focused on measurement and accountability.

Vision and Mission

We aren't the first to acknowledge that while almost every organization has a vision statement, not every organization has a clear vision. We are also aware that many districts have a vision statement because they think they ought to have one, not because it drives the work of the organization in any meaningful way. Or perhaps they have a vision and want it to drive the work but don't know how to make that happen.

Our experience of a typical district's vision and mission is that their relationship to the day-to-day operations of the district isn't clear. Instead, they tend to be written as grand statements that try to summarize the contributions of participants in community meetings or board retreats. We don't mean to suggest that those contributions aren't important; rather, we think it should be clear that the vision and the mission are the first step in designing strategy, not just summaries of community values. We aren't playing down the role of visions or missions or community values—quite the opposite, in fact. We want everyone in the organization to know how their work is informed by the vision of the district, and for the community to see their values reflected in students' experience of school. To do so, we recommend a series of elements that should be included in the vision and then turn our attention to the mission.

Vision

The vision should clearly signal that equity is an important driver of district activities. As such, it should be clear that the district fully expects that all students and their differentiated needs are included and addressed in the district's work.

The vision should also communicate what is most important for students to learn while they are in school. Wiggins and McTighe (2007) point out that many vision statements have a lot in common: "These statements can be reduced to one encompassing sentence: Schools exist to cause learning that is intellectually vital, generative of future self-directed learning, personally meaningful and productive, and socially valuable" (p. 12). Of course, there is nothing wrong with such a vision. We *do* want learning to be intellectually vital, we *do* want students to be lifelong learners, and we *do* want to create productive citizens. And in addition to the qualities that Wiggins and McTighe highlight, a district vision designed today generally includes requirements that students be able to work in teams, have excellent communications skills, be emotionally and socially adept, be comfortable and competent users of technology, and be able to appreciate and work in an increasingly diverse world. We believe it is not important that a district's vision be unique, but rather that it drives the everyday work of the district.

We also recommend that is built upon a statement of the knowledge, skills, and dispositions students should possess when they graduate high school, rather than a catch-all blend of vision, mission, beliefs, and values (i.e., a portrait of the graduate). Many districts have created, or are creating, such a portrait of a graduate, and Figure 3.2 provides a brief protocol for doing so.

Many districts have capitalized on this portrait by making it not just a high school effort but substituting the portrait for their current district vision statement. This is helpful for two reasons: the portrait of the graduate, done well, creates the clarity needed to drive a powerful strategy, and the development of the knowledge, skills, and dispositions that all students should acquire can't be accomplished solely during the final four years of school. Ambitious and meaningful outcomes for students are worth working toward as soon as students start their academic careers.

Mission

Vision and mission are often spoken of in the same breath, almost as if just one word. And indeed, many people have a hard time articulating how they differ from one another. Simply put, the vision is the end and the mission is the means. At one level, the mission of any district is simple: to fulfill the vision. But it might also include a statement about how this is to be done. In other words, the mission of the district is to ensure that all students possess those characteristics described in the portrait of the graduate by providing rich, engaging, and challenging educational experiences to all students, every day.

In our experience, both vision and mission statements can become complicated and burdensome, and frequently lists of value statements and core beliefs are appended that make it harder to determine what teachers and leaders are supposed to be paying attention to. We encourage you to strive for simplicity and clarity in articulating the vision and the mission.

Creating a Portrait of a Graduate
A tool for boards and superintendents to design a process

Begin with these initial considerations:

1. Decide whether there are any purposes other than creating the "north star" for instruction—for example, do you want to use the process as an opportunity to educate the community about progressive ideas in education? Is it politically important that the community be heavily involved in the process?

2. Is there a timeline that makes sense? For example, do you want to finish the process before the "expiration date" on your current strategic plan, so that the Portrait of a Graduate is in place before you start a major new planning process?

Based on those answers, decide:

3. The process you will use to create a Portrait of a Graduate, including what the final product will look like, and how feedback will be garnered from the larger community.

4. What needs to be communicated to whom about the purpose of the Portrait of the Graduate, the process, and the timeline?

5. Who is going to lead the process? For example, it could be a central office leader, the curriculum team, a design team comprised of internal and external stakeholders.

6. Which stakeholder groups must be represented? The process must include representation across the demographic make-up of the district.

During the process, bear in mind:

7. The Portrait of a Graduate is not an end in itself; its purpose is to provide clarity about the aspirations of the community for its children, and therefore it is only the first step in designing a strategy.

8. The process should not be unmoored from other work in the district. Here are some examples of what should be shared with the design team: if the leadership team is reading a book to inform their leadership or instructional decisions; if there are plans to increase capacity for instructional technology; if there have been discussions about changing policies such as grading or graduation requirements; if there are data showing gaps in opportunity, experience and outcome between student groups.

9. Not everyone can come to a meeting. What other opportunities can you provide to allow stakeholders to provide input? Not all of these should require access to technology.

10. We live in a rapidly changing world. What resources can you provide to the design team and/or stakeholders to help them understand how the educational and career landscape is shifting?

After the Portrait of the Graduate is complete:

11. How will you mark completion of the process and adoption of the Portrait of the Graduate?

12. How will you communicate to the community not only that the Portrait of the Graduate has been adopted, but also how it is being used to design strategy for the district to ensure all students attain the Portrait of the Graduate?

Connecticut Center for School Change. Used with permission

Figure 3.2 Creating a Portrait of a Graduate

Goals

Almost all the districts we have worked with struggle with how to set goals. We think that's because they are not clear on the purpose of goals. This is perfectly understandable. What has been written about goals frequently obscures their purpose and function. In this section, we'll attempt to clarify the purposes and functions of goals and how you can deploy them most profitably. Depending on how you use and frame them, goals can have many different purposes, including:

- Communicating values.
- Focusing attention on what is important.
- Inspiring people to work toward something.
- Designing strategy.
- Promoting changes in behavior and building of capacity.
- Helping to make decisions about how to allocate resources.
- Figuring out how to structure accountability.
- Deciding how to measure success.

When people are unclear about the purpose of goals, conflicts arise that appear to be about values when they are in fact just misunderstandings about the goals. For example, a common problem we encounter when districts are setting targets such as graduation rates is disagreement between those who want to set the goal as 100% graduation and those who want to set a target they believe is attainable within the timeframe of the plan.

The argument for setting the target at 100% is usually about values. Defenders of the goal are often upset that anyone would argue with it, as doing so implies to them that it's OK to allow some students to fall by the wayside. Proponents of any target of less than 100% are not, in fact, arguing that it's OK for some students drop out. They understand the goal to be about accountability and measurement, and perhaps also they don't want people to be discouraged when the goal is not met.

From a strategy perspective, the actual numerical target is much less important. What matters for strategy is knowing what the organization believes is most important and is, therefore, willing to allocate resources, retool, and restructure each part of the organization to achieve.

Another common misunderstanding is that goals need to be SMART—Specific, Measurable, Attainable, Results-based, and Time-bound. The SMART framework comes from research on goals and motivation in the 1960s, and it was based on improving the performance of workers such as typists who, given such goals, did indeed improve their performance. However, there is a very big difference between, for example, improving words typed per minute from 50 to 60 and improving a graduation rate from 85% to 100%.

Getting a graduation rate to 100% is not a simple technical challenge. Typists generally know all they need to know to meet their targets—that's what makes the goal attainable. Teachers and leaders, on the other hand, when given a goal such as 100% graduation within five years, don't know everything they need to know to meet this goal. It is, in the language of Heifetz and Linsky (2002), an adaptive rather than a technical goal. In this case, having a goal written in a SMART format doesn't indicate what actually needs to happen to improve graduation rates, which is what really matters.

Also, and this is a point that we almost never see attended to, not everybody needs to be working toward a goal in the same way. For example, the district might adopt a goal of 100% graduation. That may be a perfectly appropriate thing to do, because the board's purposes in adopting this goal are the first four items in the list below:

- Communicating the district's values by saying that ALL students should be successful.

- Directing attention to what is important.

- Inspiring people to work toward this aspect of student success.

- Making it clear that strategy should be based on reaching this indicator of student success.

What often happens at that point is that the superintendent says to principals, in effect, "The board's goals are my goals, and my goals are your goals, so your goal is 100% graduation." But what the superintendent should be doing is focusing on the purposes toward the bottom half of the list:

- Designing strategy that describes what teachers and leaders should be doing and what capacity should be built.

- Making decisions about how to allocate resources.

- Making decisions about how to employ routines to collect data in order to improve the strategy.

How does that play out in terms of goals?

If people are being asked to do something that they don't already know how to do, a performance goal (that is, one framed in terms of a numerical target, like a SMART goal) may actually get in the way. Research shows that in these conditions, people tend to try lots of different things in quick succession, and when they don't work, they reject them and try something else. When, on the other hand, they are given a learning goal (which is just what it sounds like: a goal framed as an instruction to learn how to do something), then people proceed much more deliberately—trying something out to see if it works and learning in the attempt. The end result is that they are much more likely to be able to do what the strategy requires of them and, therefore, to get better results than if they were given a performance goal.

Equity as a primary value of the school district should show up in its goals. We have never seen a goal that said, "all except students of color will take algebra by ninth grade," or "AP classes will include only white students." Yet such outcomes are often the norm. Therefore, unless the district clearly communicates the goal that, for example, enrollment in AP classes will be representative of the demographic makeup of the district, and then works to address the systems and structures that created these outcomes, the inequity is likely to persist.

To sum up, the goals you set depend on what you need them to do. If you want them to communicate an ambitious vision that illustrates what the organization wants to commit to achieving, then by all means set an ambitious goal. And if you want people to employ a practice that you think is critical to achieving that vision, then give them the goal of learning how to implement it.

Theory of Action

Before we say more about strategy, we want to go back to the idea of a theory of action. As we described in Chapter 2, a theory of action is a big picture idea (hypothesis) of what work will lead to the result you want to achieve. We think this is important—it is the "ploy" part of Mintzberg's

(1987) "five Ps of Strategy." But a theory of action alone is not enough; it needs to be combined with the other elements we describe here (vision, mission, and goals) to create a strategy. You need a plan to enact your big idea (another of Mintzberg's five Ps), but we have found that the connection between a theory of action and a strategic plan is often not easy to develop, and that is why we devised the following process to make this relationship clear and explicit in the plan itself.

Developing Your Strategy

If you were to ask us to help you and your team develop a strategy, either for an entire district strategic plan or for a smaller project, here is what we would do.

Before we even schedule a meeting with you, we would ask you to think about who is going to be part of the group working on the strategy. This is for three reasons.

First, we know that people who work in different roles have different knowledge about how the system works and that the more coverage we have regarding these pools of knowledge, the better off we are likely to be when decisions need to be made.

Second, make sure that you have folks in the group who are either nay-sayers or who tend to ask the hard questions about the purpose driving your decisions ("hole-pokers"). That kind of thinking can be very useful when most leaders are optimistic and see the potential before the problems.

Third, we want to make sure, given that equity is a driver of all our strategic decisions, that the working group has adequate representation of and advocates for different groups, particularly those who are historically marginalized.

In essence, we want to help you make sure your decisions are as informed and thoughtful as possible.

The next step would be to work on building out your vision, mission, and goals. We would begin the meeting by setting norms of how we would collectively work in the space. Then we would shift to talk about how we are most interested in helping you to capture your thinking about what needs to happen to achieve the mission. We would try to de-emphasize the need to properly fill in a template or make the end product look a particular way. We are not shooting for one "right answer"; rather, we believe in equifinality—there are many ways to get to our destination. To that end, we would put chart paper around the room with these titles (or similar ones, depending on the language used in your organization):

- Portrait of the graduate
- High-quality instruction
- Learning for teachers
- Coaching/instructional leadership action
- Learning for coaches
- Leadership action
- Learning for leaders

You'll notice that these titles are in the order you would expect them to be in for backward planning (and therefore the opposite of the order you would expect for implementation).

- The portrait of the graduate is the desired outcome and, once agreed upon, will become the district's vision.
- High-quality instruction is what the students need to acquire the knowledge, skills, and dispositions required in the portrait.
- Learning for teachers is what teachers need to be able to teach according to the demands of the district's definition of high-quality instruction.
- Coaching/instructional leadership describes the actions required of coaches, team leaders, and department chairs to ensure teachers acquire the knowledge and skills needed to teach the way the district requires.
- Learning for coaches/instructional leaders describes the knowledge and skills they will need to support teacher learning.
- Leadership action describes how we want formal leaders—principals, assistant principals, curriculum directors, etc.—to lead to ensure that coaches and teacher leaders get what they need to support teachers.
- Learning for leaders describes the knowledge and skills they will need to do that. (Frequently, we separate building leadership from central

office leadership and add charts that specify what central office leaders need to do and learn. Sometimes the superintendent has her own charts. We have even been asked to add charts for the board.)

As we do all this, it is worth noting that we don't take time to explain the concept of backward planning or strategy mapping to the planning team. It's not the best use of their time and can be a distraction. Instead, as quickly as possible, we get the team members into groups to fill out the charts, rotating them so that they have input on more than one chart. It may make more sense to have everybody work on the charts one at a time, in order. This works better when the group is small (fewer than six people), when participants start with very different ideas of what is important, or when the project or strategy is new and unfamiliar. In most cases, however, people already have a shared, if vague, understanding of what their goals are for students and what they think the strategy should be.

When the groups are finished (or when we run out of time), we line up the chart paper on one wall, with the chart representing the district vision of student success on the far right and the learning for leaders on the far left and the other charts in sequence in between. When lined up this way, we ask participants to find the through-line from learning for leaders all the way to student success, filling in gaps and making changes where necessary. This is often imperfect—actually, it is always imperfect—but in every district we have worked with it provides plenty of material for the team to see:

- There is broad agreement on what the district ought to be working on, which they find encouraging, because that hasn't always been clear to them.

- There is a through-line from leadership all the way to student success. In other words, they can see both the logic and the rationale of the emerging strategy.

- The requirements for each role are listed on the chart paper.

Rather than wordsmithing the words on the chart paper or making them somehow fit into a template, we type up the charts into the Disciplined

Strategy Map template. Here, we provide the completed one from Ashburn, which we will refer back to throughout the book (Figure 3.3).

As you can see, they have placed their portrait of the graduate as their vision for the district in the map.

Knowing that, in general, people are more insightful about other people than they are about themselves, we show the draft strategy map to several different groups, including perhaps instructional coaches, school secretaries, department chairs, paraeducators, parents, or the whole school faculty. We explain what has been done so far and ask them to tell us what's missing, what needs to be changed, and what connections we need to make. If we work with a group of principals, they will almost inevitably have a lot to say about what teachers ought to be doing and what central office ought to be doing, and much less about what they need to learn and do. Teachers, on the other hand, have a great deal to say about what principals need to learn and do!

We ask the people giving input on the strategy to check their work with questions such as:

- If you do all these things, will that mean that you reach your goals?
- Where does equity show up in the strategy map?

Sometimes the answer to the first question is "probably not, but that's as far as we can get right now," and that's fine. It means they know where to start and doing these things will tell them what to do next.

The answer to the second question varies a great deal depending on the district's experience to date with working on equity. Sometimes the answer comes quickly because it's obvious to them. Sometimes they must put more thought into what they're doing to make sure that ALL students acquire the characteristics described by the portrait of the graduate.

We make revisions based on their input, and that gives us a solid working draft that can be used for several purposes. As you can see in Ashburn's map, each column gives us a lot of information. For example, the column on learning for teachers is the basis for a school or district professional development plan. The column on coaching and teacher leadership helps define not only the work educators in those roles are responsible for, but also how principals must support them.

	Strategy: Deliver high quality instruction to all students to support them to reach the Vision of the Graduate; align district resources and capacity building to implement the district's definition of high-quality instruction and equity of opportunity and outcomes.		
Central office (CO) needs to learn	**Central office needs to do**	**Principals need to learn**	**Principals need to do**
How to provide more and better support to principals—to ditch the old model of hands-off supervision and move to a coaching stance. How to maximize admin meeting time—shift as much information-giving and compliance-related material to asynchronous delivery while still ensuring compliance. How to ensure teachers are using instructional resources optimally. How to model adult learning best practices in district meetings.	Provide professional learning for leaders in: ☐ Coaching ☐ Anti-racism and other equity issues. ☐ High-quality instruction (including feedback, formative assessment, classroom culture etc.) ☐ Getting feedback from staff. Curriculum audit. Materials audit. Professional learning-needs assessment. Create budget based on audits and needs assessment. Cocreate plans with building leaders for school-based professional learning and small cycles of continuous improvement. Redesign evaluation plans to encourage professional growth. Create process and stakeholder group for design of student portfolios.	Coaching skills. How to engage in conversations regarding inequity as it currently presents in school policies, programs, and behaviors. How to implement purposeful and useful feedback at all levels (students to teachers, teachers to students, coaches to teachers, teachers to coaches, etc.) Model taking risks and learning from experiments. Where to provide teachers choice on what to work on and where to insist on shared goals. Ways to promote stronger relationships among teachers and between teachers and coaches.	Provide feedback to staff in line with research on effective feedback, and in support of the district definition of high-quality instruction (as opposed to their own mental models of good instruction). Support coaches in implementing new structures for teacher learning—coaching coaches and messaging to teachers. Create or reinvent structures (e.g. collective classroom visits, weekly coaching cycles, grade-level meetings) to support teacher learning. Provide a psychologically safe workplace for trying out new practices. Assist with audits and needs assessments, both logistically and messaging and press how issues of inequity manifest. Implement plans for school-based professional learning including a centering of equity in these plans. Meet weekly with coaches.
As measured by...	**As measured by...**	**As measured by...**	**As measured by...**
Self-assessment of CO leaders.	360 feedback. Completed audits. Completed plans. Completed budget. Stakeholder meetings occur and are fully attended. PD sessions scheduled and attended by leaders.	Feedback from coaches and teachers. Self-assessment of principals—perceived self-efficacy.	Coach meetings are scheduled weekly and all coaches attend. Feedback from coaches and teachers. Data from coaches' meeting with teachers. Structures are shifted to support greater opportunities for teacher learning.

Connecticut Center for School Change. Used with permission.

Figure 3.3 Ashburn Strategy Map

Theory of Action: If all students have access to and receive high-quality instruction focused on formative assessment and feedback and curriculum driven by the Vision of the Graduate, then all students will acquire the knowledge, skills, and dispositions defined in the Vision of the Graduate

"Mezzanine" leaders need to learn	"Mezzanine" leaders need to do	Teachers need to learn	High-quality instruction	Vision of the Graduate
Research on adult learning. Data and assessment practices and tools. How to implement and effectively facilitate small cycles of continuous improvement, e.g. via working with grade-level teams. How to implement the same things that teachers are being asked to implement (i.e. powerful culture, student agency, formative assessment, feedback, etc.), but also the underlying research. How to productively engage in difficult conversations about how bias and discrimination play out in schools and the classroom as well as actions to facilitate greater opportunity and access for marginalized students.	Facilitate collective learning opportunities for teachers (e.g., PLCs, data teams, etc.) that includes centering of student work and learning how to use this data in situ. Monitor implementation of curriculum and the integration of more culturally relevant content. Provide differentiated levels of support for teachers based on their needs and expertise. This would include modeling particular instructional practices, e.g. process feedback, hinge questions, setting learning intentions, as needed. Share research on high-quality instruction. Provide professional development on relationship building with a focus on cultural competence and unpacking bias.	How to create a powerful classroom culture, including structures and routines. How to leverage relationships to stretch students personally and academically. How to embed formative assessment practices into instruction and use formative assessment as feedback to teachers. How to use learning intentions and success criteria to enable students to self-regulate. How to ensure that students receive effective feedback. How to engineer challenging tasks that increase student agency. How to minimize bias in student assessments.	Teachers create a classroom culture that is warm, supportive, challenging, and emotionally and physically safe for all students. Teachers ensure all students engage with challenging tasks with appropriate scaffolding. Teachers-embed student self-regulation into instruction, including formative assessment and feedback.	Students graduating from our district will be: Academically prepared Confident learners Socially responsible Mentally and physically healthy Effective communicators Valuable collaborators
As measured by...	As measured by...	As measured by...	As measured by...	As measured by...
Self-assessment of "mezzanine" leaders—perceived self-efficacy. All schools have access to, and are regularly implementing, formative assessments. Teachers engage in cycles of inquiry. Conversations about equity are being had and shifts occur in how students are discussed.	All schools have designated times for teachers to meet in PLCs. Sharing data on implementation during weekly meetings with principals is a norm. Feedback from teachers on modeling instruction etc.	Self-assessment of teachers—Perceived self-efficacy. Feedback on professional learning. All students show ability to successfully engage in more challenging tasks. Disproportionality in higher level courses declines.	Classroom visits by coaches/"mezzanine" leaders/principals that show full teacher implementation of these skills and evidence of students internalizing these skills in practice Student surveys of school climate are positive and do not show significant differences across identity groups.	State summative evaluations. Student portfolios. Students from traditionally minoritized groups are no longer disproportionately underrepresented in high level course and/or "feeder" courses.

Figure 3.3 (Continued)

There is one more step that Ashburn might take before deciding that they are done with the first version of their map, and that is to pressure test it. We have had a great deal of success in finding the weaknesses in a strategy by employing a variation on Gary Klein's (2007) concept of the "pre-mortem." The idea here is that a panel of stakeholders is asked to find the failings in a strategy by imagining that it has not created the intended outcomes. We include a protocol for undertaking a pre-mortem (Figure 3.4).

We encourage people to make revisions to the strategy map on a regular basis as they learn more about what it will take to reach their vision of student success, but not so frequently that it becomes impossible to keep track of the versions. We also encourage the revision of other documents so

---

Pre-Mortem Protocol
Based on the work of Gary Klein

Purpose
The pre-mortem is designed to find the flaws in a plan/strategy/theory of action BEFORE it is implemented.

Steps
Form pairs or small groups (3–5 members). You will take turns examining each other's plans. Each plan will be presented in turn and receive feedback. For each presentation, designate a presenter, a time-keeper, and a note-taker. Times are listed on the protocol, and the note-taker is charged with giving the presenter notes from the group's discussion at the end of the round (although the presenter may elect to take his/her own notes as well as, or in place of).

The pre-mortem asks you to imagine a fiasco: we are at some point in the near future, and it is clear that the strategy has failed to deliver the intended results. As our kids would say, an epic fail. Your task, then, is to generate likely causes of this failure, which could be omissions, faulty thinking, quality-control issues, or many other possible weaknesses.

1. Presenter outlines the plan as it currently stands. Ask clarifying questions of the presenter so that you are clear on the theory of action behind the plan—leave the details for later. (5 minutes)
2. Optional: Individually annotate the plan, identifying possible weaknesses and suggesting possible ways to strengthen the plan, *in order to forestall the epic fail*. (3 minutes)
3. Everyone in the group, except the presenter, shares what they noticed about the plan and its weaknesses, shares wonderings, and makes suggestions. The presenter listens, and the note-taker takes notes unless not needed by presenter. (5 minutes)
4. The presenter reflects on the feedback and thanks the other group members. (3 minutes)
5. Debrief the process and decompress. (Up to 4 minutes)
   a. How well did this process work for you?
   b. Were you able to make improvements to the plan?
   c. How else might you use this strategy?

The protocol takes 18–20 minutes per plan.

Figure 3.4 Pre-mortem Protocol

there is coherence across the district. For example, the district's definition of high-quality instruction should correspond with the district's plan for teacher evaluation and also its plan for students who need more intensive intervention.

One more thing. We are often asked about the relationship between a school plan and a district plan, or between a literacy plan and a school plan. The answer is that plans are nested; it is not possible to represent every facet of a district in a plan that spans the whole organization. But it is possible—and it is desirable—for grade level teams or high school departments to take the larger plan and create one that represents their work as it applies to that plan.

Return to Principles

In this chapter we have discussed how to think about one's district vision, mission, and goals, and provided a process for how to create these features. Before we move to the nitty-gritty of the plan and its activities, we want to highlight for you where the organizing principles show up in this chapter. We do so as a reminder to consistently return to the principles as guideposts for practice.

Equity

- Writing the vision, mission, and goals is a public opportunity for district leadership to explicitly commit to equity and policies to disrupt current discriminatory policies and systems within and across its schools. It must not be squandered.

- Equity requires not just trying to do better with what you have, but also investigating the ways current structures and systems are unjust and directly addressing them (for example, discipline approaches, the pathways to honors classes, the assignment of teachers and other resources, etc.).

- The vision of the school district must clearly apply to all students. Many districts use the phrase "all students" and some include words such as "equity" and "equitable" in their mission and vision, with aligned strategies that distribute resources toward greater areas of need.

- Goals communicate values. Goals that require disaggregation of data communicate that the performance of ALL students matters, not just achievement in the aggregate.

- The district strategy must be "audited" for equity. Will the strategy address current inequities as well as lead to equitable opportunity and achievement for all students?

Logic

- It should be clear how the district's vision, mission, goals, and strategy are connected.

- The logic of a strategy or plan should be clear and rational. Everyone should be able to see how one action leads to another via a chain of causation.

- The end result of the action required by the strategy and the plan should be the attainment of the vision.

Capacity

- People can only be expected to do what they know how to do. Every strategy and every plan require action; therefore, every strategy and every plan must pay close attention to what people need to know and be able to do to complete the action required in the plan.

Coherence

- The strategy map is the best tool we know of for creating coherence, because it makes transparent how people in different roles in the organization are connected to a common vision.

References

Battelle for Kids. (2018). Portrait of a graduate: A first step in transforming your school system. Retrieved May 23, 2020, from https://portraitofa-graduate.org/

Heifetz, R. A., & Linsky, M. (2002). *Leadership on the line: Staying alive through the dangers of leading*. Boston, MA: Harvard Business School Press.

Klein, G. (2007). Performing a project premortem. *Harvard Business Review, 85*(9), 18–19.

Mintzberg, H. (1987). The strategy concept: Five Ps for strategy. *California Management Review, 30*(1), 11–24.

Wiggins, G. P., & McTighe, J. (2005). *Understanding by design* (expanded 2nd ed.). Alexandria, VA: Association for Supervision and Curriculum Development.

Wiggins, G. P., & McTighe, J. (2007). *Schooling by design: Mission, action, and achievement*. Alexandria, VA: ASCD

4 | Leadership and Creating Conditions for Success

Questions about what the district needed to work on produced responses. All this was very helpful. The truly eye-opening part, however, was what Maria learned about others' perceptions of her leadership. She learned, for example, that she was widely regarded as a strong instructional leader; the educators in her district clearly believed that she was well grounded in curriculum, instruction, assessment, social-emotional learning, and coaching.

At the same time, comments that focused on areas of growth such as her needing to "learn how to create coherence," "create conditions to focus and sustain work on instruction," and "build a budget and find resources" were made. Maria discovered through follow-up conversations that these remarks may have had to do with her predecessor's lack of focus or follow-through on the management side of the superintendency. People were going to be playing close attention to whether Maria could align the district's educational infrastructure with the vision.

With these new insights in mind, Maria began to work more closely with the principals to find out what they needed from the district to move forward with a plan.

Chapter Overview

In the last chapter we introduced the Disciplined Strategy Map and showed how district and school leaders might work together to set a direction for the district (that is, develop a vision, mission, and goals) as well as engage in backward mapping to facilitate a theory of action. Together, these elements become the district's Disciplined Strategic Plan for improvement. In this chapter, we focus on leadership at the district and school levels, and how this leadership is connected to the plan.

If you are following along with the blank template of the Disciplined Strategy Map or Ashburn's map (and we suggest that you do use one of these), the six left-hand columns (those that focus on the central office, principals, and mezzanine leaders) will be the focus of this chapter. In Chapter 5, we will focus on the right-hand side of the map, and specifically the work of teachers engaging in high-quality instruction. In thinking about the relationship between the different sides of the map, we can understand the items on the left as being focused on leaders' creating the conditions to best enable teachers to learn and grow and thus to engage in more effective and high-quality instruction to better meet all students' needs (the right-hand side of the map).

Indeed, though we have strong opinions about leadership (what it should be and where it lives—e.g., relationships as well as positions), we narrow our focus here to the conditions that leaders in education—formal and informal—can create to enable the success of the strategy (in Ashburn's case, leveraging high-quality instruction for continuous improvement) and to ensure it aligns with, and is deeply rooted in, the principles of Equity, Logic, Coherence, and Capacity. Such activities are, of course, just one slice of educational leadership. We don't pretend otherwise. But we see this slice as critical, complex, and needing attention.

We focus on what we call educational infrastructure, or, as Mehta and Fine (2015) describe it, the purposes and practices that work in concert to support schooling. Of course, this is a broad definition and includes everything related to what happens in all classrooms. To help us get slightly narrower, we might categorize these different purposes and practices as falling under culture, resources, and structures.

We will discuss how these elements should be deployed by district leadership to support schools and create the conditions necessary to support the development and enactment of their Disciplined Strategic Plan, drawing connections to Ashburn's experiences and actions where appropriate. We will also address how principals and "mezzanine" level leaders—those who serve as intermediaries between teachers and principals (for example, teacher leaders, coaches, and those in similar roles)—work in concert to ensure effective conditions for teachers and students to learn and grow.

A Strategic Leadership Stance

In our model of Disciplined Strategic Planning, much of the work of leadership will end up in writing. Regardless of your planning format, the presence of some leadership characteristics will increase the chances of success, whether or not they are ever included in the plan or written down. We know that some of the ideas below will not appear in writing—in your plan or anywhere else. They are important nonetheless.

First, as we described as part of Ashburn's process in Chapter 3, leaders actively engage in all parts of the planning process as cocreators, rather than delegators. For some, this way of working may already be in place.

For others, working alongside colleagues as colearners may feel new and perhaps uncomfortable. This approach is important because all roles are important in developing strategy. Setting one above another limits leaders' view of the whole.

We see leaders' roles as creating the necessary educational infrastructure to support continuous improvement. This means district leaders need to know the current state of the district's schools regarding Equity, Logic, Coherence, and Capacity, and principals need to know the same about their schools. Such knowledge requires an understanding of both the meaning of these principles and what they look like in action. If this understanding isn't complete, districts may need to conduct audits across and within its schools, including, for example, an equity audit (Skrla, et al., 2009) as mentioned in Chapter 2, a curriculum audit (English, 2000), or a professional development needs assessment (Marshall, 2016).

Additionally, it's more important for leaders to model a learner stance than it is for them to demonstrate deep expertise. Absolute expertise, while perhaps a commendable goal, isn't possible, nor is it particularly desirable. It's better for leaders to act as expert learners: people who are willing to say "I don't know" and to constantly seek out new and better ideas while doing their best with the knowledge, skills, and resources available to them.

While accountability is part of this model, it's a reciprocal form of accountability in which the district leaders expect educators to meet only outcomes and processes for which schools are fully supported in achieving. In Disciplined Strategic Planning, district and school leaders ask educators to meet particular goals but also ask themselves to provide the necessary resources to create aligned systems, structures, and cultures.

In such a district, those at the central office take responsibility for ensuring there's adequate infrastructure to allow schools to focus on what they have control over in the context of the everyday interactions of educators, students, families, and the larger community. This means the district sees its role as supportive and oriented toward capacity building and not toward compliance and deadlines. Sometimes this entails a reconceptualization of the senior leadership team's mental model of their relationship with school leaders: instead of seeing the district's primary responsibility as holding principals accountable, they shift to thinking of themselves as existing in support of principals, teachers, students, families, and the community.

There will also be a need to recruit others beyond the principal to engage in the learning process. In particular, there will be a need for district leaders and principals to help mezzanine-level leaders, including others on the administrative team and teacher leaders, to build and support the plan and each of its components.

We don't mean leadership should simply give mezzanine leaders a mandate for improvement. Rather, this approach means providing the resources, structures, and culture to ensure mezzanine leaders can share their expertise and make decisions regarding local implementation. For example, they should weigh in on the relationship between the district plan and local needs regarding content and specific goals. They would then take charge of implementing these efforts and ongoing monitoring routines.

Creating Enabling Conditions for Schools

Let's talk about some of the infrastructure considerations district and school leaders should be focused on regarding Disciplined Strategic Planning and leadership. What culture, resources, and structures need to be in place?

While the elements we discuss here don't cover all possibilities, we highlight some of the ones we view as most critical. Again, though we treat these conditions as discrete, they are, of course, deeply entwined. As such, we ask you to treat the following not as a checklist but as guideposts to help keep you headed in the right direction. Moreover, these elements depend heavily on context and so while we provide examples, it's possible (and probable) that each school in a district may have different and/or overlapping needs.

Needs, whether they exist at the district, school, or individual teacher or student level, are likely to be unearthed as well as evolve over time as the work unfolds. For example, we have worked on supporting the improvement efforts of districts that identified differentiated instruction as a problem and, in response, introduced data teams to support teachers' ability and skill with student data. Doing so, they quickly found the district lacked standards-aligned, formative assessment tools, and many of the teachers had little idea about how to run an effective team. In such a case, the resources, structure, and culture originally directed toward curriculum adoption may need to be redirected toward building infrastructure around assessment (tech support, assessment identification and adoption, data analysis support, etc.) and localized support for teams (teacher leaders, money to pay for coverage for teachers to meet, new norms for working together, etc.).

We understand that a variety of things could fall under each of these categories. We offer these elements as a start to the rich, ongoing conversations you will undoubtedly have as you engage in this process.

Culture

The research on leadership and how it can be leveraged to facilitate continuous improvement tells us that attending to organizational culture is some of the most important work leaders can do. Ed Schein (2004), in the book *Organizational Culture and Leadership*, describes two dimensions of culture:

- The shared assumptions among members of an organization that may be invisible, but which manifest in the behaviors of those individuals;
- The systems and structures that stimulate and hinder behaviors.

The role of leadership is thus to replace the default culture with a set of beliefs and practices focused on continuous improvement. The case studies provided in these well-known books on organizational improvement—*The Culture Code* (Coyle, 2018), *An Everyone Culture* (Kegan & Lahey, 2016), and *The Fearless Organization* (Edmondson, 2018)—reinforce the crucial role leadership plays in developing an organizational environment in which people can speak up, take risks, and learn.

While it's outside the scope of this book for us to review all of the research on the features of an effective culture and what leaders should do to create it, we want to point out some that we think are critical to the success of a Disciplined Strategic Plan.

Demanding an Unrelenting Orientation Toward Equity and Justice

The pursuit of equity and justice should be at the core of all improvement efforts. While this may sound straightforward, research makes clear that educators often have difficulty committing to this work.

Part of this has to do with the way white, middle-class values are perpetuated as the norm in schools, often by an educational force that is white and middle class, and often positioning those who do not represent these identities (i.e., many of the students) as deficient. Structural inequities and discrimination then go relatively untroubled and are replicated over time. It's up to educational leaders to ask critical questions about how the day-to-day, taken-for-granted practices of the school may be reinforcing inequity, and then work to change them.

In Ashburn, this process began with Superintendent Jenkins asking different communities about their experiences in the district's schools and by engaging in an equity audit to see how well the current policies, practices, and structures were serving all kids. The map reflects these efforts, and an orientation toward building equity, with the far left column focused on what the central office needs to learn. In it, Ashburn's leadership clarifies that central office leaders will need to actively engage in examining and critiquing current ways of doing their work to ensure they are living up to its mission, vision, and goals. It does not make the presumption that these skills exist or that they can be enhanced to without new learning. If you follow across the columns, you then see how a focus on equity manifests across the plan, with training and support to facilitate more reflective leaders who examine and begin to address their bias and how it operates in schools, and who learn how to create opportunities and spaces for others to do the same. These efforts show up, for example, in the column dedicated to what mezzanine leaders need to learn. As it states in the plan, "mezzanine leaders need to learn:"

> How to productively engage in difficult conversations about how bias and discrimination play out in schools and the classroom as well as actions to facilitate greater opportunity and access for marginalized students. (see Figure 3.3)

These efforts would then create the conditions to support teachers to engage in instructional practices that are culturally competent and to build relationships with students grounded in love and an asset orientation (the right side of the map). It is important here to mention, and is revealed in the map, that these activities do not happen in a vacuum. As we discuss below, efforts aimed at equity are coupled with larger cultural shifts and structures aimed at creating better collaboration, relationships, and trust—all essential elements for making real change.

Here, we want to emphasize again that while the map can help set you on your way, leading for equity is not easy, both because it's new to many and because talking about uncomfortable things, and race in particular, is hard to do and requires an ability to tolerate conflict and uncertainty. This is not the norm in schools nor among white people generally (Robin DiAngelo's book *White Fragility* [2018], provides insight into why.) There are a number of excellent and growing resources to support these efforts, such as *Everyday Antiracism* (Pollock, 2008), *How to be an Anti-Racist* (Kendi, 2019) and *Courageous Conversations About Race* (Singleton, 2014), etc. We encourage educators of all backgrounds, and white educators particularly, to study and talk about these texts and other issues related to race, including whiteness and white supremacy, as well as other forms of discrimination, with one another as part of any improvement effort.

Fostering Collective Accountability

Another cultural norm leaders need to foster in the context of Disciplined Strategic Planning is collective accountability. In this model, educators share specific expectations and values about their work, and hold each other and themselves to these expectations to produce positive results for students. This means a shift away from the culture of accountability currently preferred in our educational system—that which focuses predominantly on a narrow group of performance outcomes—and toward the process of learning and sustainability.

Making this shift requires a general and agreed-upon sense of what good processes look like in practice. In the case of Ashburn public schools, for example, to effectively create a sense of internal accountability toward a particular process and the goal of every child receiving high-quality instruction, educators must share the following understandings:

- What high-quality instruction looks like regarding their particular content area focus (see Chapter 5).
- What the expectation is for students in response to such instruction.

Our focus on equity also requires a simultaneous discussion about how bias (unconscious or otherwise) might be playing out in teachers' expectations. The commitment to collaborative work, creating time and infrastructure to support the discussion and analysis of student work, and professional development could all be used to support these efforts and can be seen in various places in Ashburn's plan.

Elmore (2005) makes the case that internal accountability thrives when demands for change are coupled with the support necessary to make these changes. This premise is applicable around tangible resources as well as the more intangible aspect of role modeling. To make internal accountability a reality, leaders need to consistently act in ways that show they are accountable to their colleagues. Teachers and others are very sensitive to discrepancies between what leaders say they value and what they actually do. For example, if a school leader says everyone is responsible to each other but then fails to show up for teachers with resources and other forms of support, the leader will lose credibility and the sense of internal accountability will be diminished.

Embracing Distributed Leadership

Formal leaders interested in making real change will need to build a culture in which all members of the community can engage in shared, collaborative, or distributed leadership. Shared leadership requires thinking of leadership not as something that is linked to a position ("She is the principal, therefore She is a leader"), but rather as actions taken by those attending to the well-being and growth of the organization, such as being part of a Professional Learning Community (PLC), starting a community outreach effort, supporting colleagues with their practice, or any one of many activities designed to help the organization meet its goals. Leaders are those who are willing to step up and take action, rather than those anointed with a particular job title.

Our key premise is this: the organization's strategy will be stronger if the educators implementing the strategy are involved in its development. Moreover, as frontline workers, teachers have a great deal of insight into what principals and district leaders ought to do; asking them for their insights while designing a strategy only makes sense. This puts teachers in the position of providing input to help strengthen the strategy and make implementation smoother, rather than having to point out what isn't working and why during implementation.

In practice, creating a culture of shared leadership means that part of the formal leaders' role is to create structures that facilitate teachers' opportunities to come together to collaborate and plan. It also means ensuring that decision-making, whenever possible, is a team activity. Shared decision-making entails processes that allow for broad participation in the design of school policy.

In Ashburn, we can see the creation of such structures in the central office's plan to cocreate plans with building leaders for school-based professional learning and small cycles of continuous improvement. These efforts are then mirrored by school leaders in the plan with the development or reinvention of structures (e.g., collective classroom visits, weekly coaching cycles, grade-level meetings) to support teacher learning. These are coupled with training for leaders so that these structures are truly collaborative in orientation and support shared leadership.

Implied here is that shared decision-making requires principals and others in designated leadership positions to give away power they have traditionally held. Also, shared leadership is not merely the delegation of administrative tasks and duties such as supervising lunch, creating the master schedule, and writing curriculum (although the performance of these tasks can be shared, just as decision-making can be shared). To ensure leadership is not focused solely on the delegation of administrative tasks, the district may need to also create structures to help principals by lessening their administrative demands and providing them political coverage and possibly professional development.

Engaging in Continuous Improvement and Psychological Safety

The role of leadership is to create a culture of continuous improvement. Technical knowledge is crucial, but just as important is the understanding that there is no pure technical solution to problems that involve multiple variables (including people) interacting in unpredictable ways. The road to success, then, is to start with a strategy that represents the organization's best guess about what will work (including the capacity and conditions needed), try to make it work, and then take forward the lessons learned from the successes and failures. In other words, to quote the title of Edmondson and Verdin's 2017 piece in the Harvard Business Review, "Strategy is a hypothesis you constantly adjust." This approach is also known as action research, PDSA (plan, do, study, act), and continuous improvement. The phrase "learning organization" is frequently used to describe organizations that manage to put into practice their best guesses and learn from the successes and failures of trying to do that.

One important element in this process, and a piece of additional wisdom from Edmondson (2002), is the need to create a culture of psychological safety. As she explains, an organization can be considered psychologically safe when those within it view the environment as conducive to interpersonally risky behaviors like speaking up or asking for help. In such environments people are more likely to "unfreeze" from previous patterns of behavior and grow and learn. To support such efforts, leaders need to acknowledge their own fallibility and proactively seek input from others, as well as maintain mutual support and acceptance. The shared leadership structures we mentioned earlier can also be utilized for this purpose.

With such structures as part of their plan, we can see Ashburn taking steps to build these cultural norms. In the column dedicated to what principals need to do, we see an explicit statement prioritizing psychological safety. However, these words do not stand alone: throughout the left-hand columns, there is a clear emphasis on helping leaders build stronger and deeper relationships with their colleagues, as well as on modeling fallibility and openness to change—important elements in building a culture of safety and continuous improvement.

Having Strategic Conversations

The ability to have meaningful and clear conversations is an undervalued leadership skill. Having the skills to interact with fellow educators is crucial in developing strategy, because good strategy depends on a wide range of stakeholders not just volunteering their input, but also being asked for their input in a systematic way and feeling safe to say what they really think. The creation of a map that emphasizes coherence and transparency, as seen in Ashburn, can be understood as an essential step toward this level and type of communication.

Leaders must also be attentive to communicating regularly and often. The only way to reach a shared understanding is to have repeated, in-depth conversations during which the meaning of terms such as engagement, differentiation, equity, developmental, rigor, and accountability are explored and challenged. This is important in creating strategy because it's too easy to decide that a district is going to focus on an instructional practice, such as student-centered learning, and have a sizable portion of the teachers believe that they have nothing to learn and don't have to change anything about the way they teach because their instruction is already student-centered.

Resources

Financial Resources

Financial leadership is the creation of viable budgets that support the efforts in the Disciplined Strategy Plan at all levels. An unfunded mandate is not acceptable, nor is the heavy allocation of resources to only one area of the improvement strategy. Given the state of funding for schools and districts, the reallocation of resources may also be necessary to support the strategic plan. Again, we don't expect anyone to do "more with less," too many are already doing exactly that.

With that said, it's also important to shift the plan if you don't have the financial resources needed to support it. Such shifts are not necessarily negative and can serve to enhance capacity. For example, rather than hiring external professional developers to work with all teachers, a district or school could pay for some teacher leaders to be trained and then give them a stipend or alleviation of their teaching duties so they can support their colleagues in real time to build those same skills. With constrained financial resources, district leaders may want to shift away from sending money out of the system and toward building internal capacity. Put simply, budget decisions need to be understood as strategic decisions and vice versa. This is why, in Ashburn, and we believe should be true in all districts' plans, there is explicit reference to the budget and its connection to identified needs. Doing so helps to provide a constant reminder to all stakeholders of the symbiotic relationship between the budget and the strategy, and decisions regarding resource allocations should not be made without considering this connection.

We want to remind you about the principles that make our approach disciplined: Equity, Logic, Coherence, and Capacity. Budget deliberations need to be driven by these principles. This may create some difficult but necessary conversations about differentiated resource allocations for certain schools, teachers, students, etc. To make things equitable, some will need more than others. These difficult conversations define leadership as they require integrity and courage, and they change the trajectory of innumerable students for years to come.

Human Resources

Resources can also be understood as the people who fulfill the various roles and supports to make the district and schools run. It's critical that leaders attend to human resources when building out and implementing their plan. This means ensuring the right people with the right knowledge and skills are in the right positions, or, if opportunities are more constrained, that those in such positions are being adequately trained (with resources gathered by the district) to build such capabilities.

Consistent with how we define the relationship between districts and schools for Disciplined Strategic Planning, these capabilities will and should be focused on helping prepare principals and mezzanine leaders to learn alongside their teachers as facilitators and/or coaches—skills which must be attended to and cultivated over time and should be, as seen in Ashburn, addressed throughout the plan. Similar to our suggested leadership actions regarding financial resources, effective leadership regarding human resources may also require reallocation of resources to ensure there is equitable distribution of the most effective and skilled educators across and within all district schools.

Physical Resources

Other resources leaders need to consider and address to create the conditions necessary for a Disciplined Strategic Plan to be successful are physical ones. Such resources could include facilities issues such as appropriate access to the internet, adequate classroom libraries, and shared spaces within the school free of hazardous materials and with well-regulated temperature controls.

It also means teachers and other educators and support staff have the materials necessary to do their work. This may mean books, curriculum guides, laptops for students, or simply enough paper and pencils. Also, as is true in Ashburn's plan, it means that leaders provide assessment tools that facilitate teachers' ability to get quick, easy-to-use, and meaningful formative data on student growth toward the defined goal. At the school level, it may also mean finding a space that can be officially designated for teachers to congregate in teams where they have access to the necessary materials and without interruption.

Structures

When we talk about structures, we're talking about all the organizational routines, processes, laws, and policies that serve to dictate, compel, or cajole schools and school systems to behave in particular ways.

For example, the evaluation process is a structure because it defines the parameters of effective instructional practices. So too, the school calendar and how classes and students get assigned are structures that largely define teachers' and students' daily lives and work in school. Laws about how students with disabilities are served or those pertaining to student discipline may be other structures one could look at to understand how the work in schools is understood and enacted.

Given that broad definition, you may be wondering how to attend to all these structures in creating your plan. As you consider your plan in relation to your goals, there may be some structures that are more salient than others. We recommend you attend to those first with a continual eye to the way other prominent structures may play a role in your efforts, and intervene when necessary.

We focus on routines more in Chapter 6; here, we would just like to point out that it is easy to underestimate the power of routines. They have a tendency to become part of the furniture, so to speak. A key leadership move is to exploit routines to build the capacity of those who participate in them. The way to do this is by embedding "teachable moments," giving the participants real work to do, and providing information about how well the strategy is working (which is what we go into more deeply in Chapter 6) to improve the strategy.

Hiring, Supervision, and Evaluation

Reviewing and attending to district and school structures relating to the professional pipeline and individuals' ability to enter, succeed, and grow within it are critical to the success of your plan. For example, if the hiring process is too laborious or inefficient (which it often is in many districts) it will be very difficult to get mission-critical staff in the places where they're needed most. Moreover, when people are placed in new positions, or in old ones where they're asked to do new things, supervision structures need to work to provide the necessary professional support, guidance, and resources. This means those fulfilling such roles need to be skilled and that the processes for receiving such support are relatively straightforward, equitable, and transparent. Principal supervisors have a distinct role that is centered on instructional improvement. They take a coaching stance toward the principals they serve, helping them identify problems of practice, generate ideas and possibilities, work with their teams, collect and reflect on data from a variety of sources, and seek feedback on their actions. Principal supervisors must be clear that they're acting in service of the district's plan, and not as ambassadors for their own experience of what works. Doing so will help principals as they attempt to get teachers to engage with these practices and to have mezzanine leaders serve as instructional leaders in the building.

Finally, as Ashburn points out in its plan, evaluation systems need to be aligned with the theory of action undergirding the strategy and incent learning behaviors among adults. While it's perhaps unrealistic to think the entire evaluation system will be changed as a result of the strategic plan, it may be useful to consider how processes such as teacher performance goals may be reframed or restructured to allow for greater risk-taking and learning. For example, goals could be measured in terms of growth and ability to change relative to feedback rather than student proficiency levels. Doing so may move teachers away from choosing what are perhaps more easily attainable goals and toward those which push them to learn and improve.

Schedule and Calendar

Other important structures for leaders to consider are the schedule and calendar. While it's essential to build human capital to support enhanced practice, if teachers aren't given adequate time to share that capital it will go to waste.

As is clear in Ashburn's plan, part of the leaders' work is to think creatively about creating more uninterrupted time for teachers to meet with one another and with mezzanine-level leaders. This may mean considering shifts to the calendar so that teachers are given time during the regular workday to meet (for example, bimonthly early release days for students). We recommend blocks of at least 45-minutes of teacher collaborative time for it to be meaningful.

Teachers will also need to feel assured that their kids are being well attended to and learning is occurring during these teacher collaborative blocks. It may take some creativity to ensure all kids are getting high-quality instruction during this time.

Beyond teacher meetings, it's also important to create times for mezzanine leaders to meet regularly with administrators and for school administrators to meet with district leaders. Again, these meetings need to be purposeful, uninterrupted, and organized in such a way that participants feel their work at their schools is being well attended to while at the meeting.

Standards and Curriculum

Another structural element that needs to be attended to by leaders is the alignment between the standards, the curriculum, and the district's portrait of a graduate (see Chapter 3 for more on this process). It's not so very long since the textbooks issued to students were the only curriculum, and it's still the case that in many schools and districts, curriculum is either missing, outdated, or not intentionally aligned to the districts' portrait of the graduate. In light of what is known about implicit bias in education and its relationship to low expectations for students of color and students from poverty, leaders have an obligation to ensure the taught curriculum represents and will result in high achievement for all students.

In Ashburn, as highlighted in their plan, meeting this obligation began with the central office's commitment to an all-school curriculum audit coupled with an equity audit. It then manifested in school- and district-based discussions on the definition of high-quality instruction (more on this in Chapter 5), as well as the supporting mezzanine leaders monitoring instruction and helping teachers incorporate culturally relevant and sustaining materials into their classes.

For many districts with an ambitious portrait of the graduate, another early step in their strategy, and thus appearing in their plan (see Ashburn's Disciplined Strategy Map [Figure 3.3] for more), would be to include a step for those in the district to write learning progressions for each strand of their vision. These learning progressions describe what students will learn at each grade level or grade band (such as K through first or fifth through eighth). Leaders need to make sure teachers at these grade levels coordinate with one another to ensure there are neither overlaps nor gaps in the progression of students in each core skill or knowledge area from grade level to grade level.

Once the curriculum is in place, the district can turn its attention to developing an instructional model that is intended to ensure all students acquire the content and competencies described in the portrait of the graduate. We believe that districts should promote a streamlined definition of instruction, for reasons that we explore in more depth in Chapter 5.

Student Discipline and Behavior

Research repeatedly shows that students of color are still disproportionately disciplined (formally and informally) at alarming rates. An audit of behavioral and discipline systems and how they function relative to all children's opportunities to equitably access and excel with the material is necessary in any strategic plan and can be addressed via a good equity audit, as used in Ashburn. Moreover, we argue it's worthwhile to press all educators to examine how their beliefs are contributing to inequitable outcomes for students and how current student behavior and discipline structures may play a role in that process. This investigation should extend to how parents are treated in the system and the degree to which they are treated as real partners in their child's learning and development.

Finally, it's worth noting that even if racial or other kinds of disparities don't seem prevalent in the school's behavior/discipline data, it doesn't mean that these structures are fair or equitable. We say this as we have both worked with educators from predominantly white-serving districts who have said that issues of equity don't apply to them due to the demographics of their students. This is false. Whiteness is a racial identity and needs to be unpacked and critically examined. Other forms of discrimination—ableism, homophobia, gender discrimination, etc.—all require our attention too. Behavioral codes, whether regarding honor or dress, all have built-in assumptions about what is "normal," "proper," or "appropriate" that tend to favor hegemonic notions of identity. For example, codes regarding hairstyles are often highly gendered and racialized, thereby disproportionately punishing girls and/or Black children. These codes then tell students and their families what and who is most valued at the school. As such, they also deserve attention and critique.

Student Data and Reporting

While we will discuss issues related to ongoing assessment and measurement more in Chapter 6, we thought it worth mentioning the need for leaders to attend to structures that facilitate the ability for the district, schools, and individual educators to have timely, useful, and valuable data from which to make decisions.

These data may be anything from attendance numbers to behavioral referrals to student scores on standards-aligned, benchmark assessments to "exit tickets" from a classroom. To support educators' use of these data sources, it's important for leaders to invest in things like effective data management systems, formative assessment tools that help to ensure teacher efforts are aligned with state and district goals, and human beings who can understand, interpret, and present data in digestible ways.

Return to Principles

Leadership is the driver of Disciplined Strategic Planning and the changes that take place as a result. Below we highlight how our vision for leadership is deeply grounded in our principles and the implications such grounding has for leaders' day-to-day work in schools.

Equity

- Equity should be the ultimate driver and goal of leadership and any plan for improvement. This will need to be lived by leaders every single day. It's hard work that requires deep and critical reflection, knowledge, tools, and grace. It's everyone's responsibility and if it's not at the center, it's not happening to the degree it needs to.

- Leaders should understand from the onset of their planning that they will have to give different kinds of infrastructure supports and amounts to different groups based on need.

- As we already live in an inequitable system, it's important for leaders to acknowledge and think about these issues from the beginning. An essential part of doing equity work and leadership is upsetting taken-for-granted ways of doing things and considering how what we consider "normal" practice may actually favor certain groups over others or send messages about the relative worth of certain cultures and ways of being.

Logic

- Leadership requires thoughtful initial planning that facilitates opportunities to meet the demands of the plan, measure progress, and adjust accordingly. A strong logic model provides opportunities for this to occur.

- Logic moves leaders to think deeply about how they will measure and adjust their plan over time. It also suggests the need to have systems to support measurement and evaluation that are aligned with the goals of the organizations (more about this in Chapter 6).

Capacity

- Leadership for Disciplined Strategic Planning requires an understanding that capacity for change and improvement sits across all features of educational infrastructure (culture, resources, and structures). Moreover, leaders understand that this capacity is dynamic and can shift over time.

- Leaders must know the current level of capacity across the organization. This will take work and requires both initial audits and continual monitoring across the system.

- Leaders understand that educators can only do as much as they have the capacity for. If the conditions don't enable people to do their best work, the plan will not be fully effective.

- Leaders recognize that by taking the time to invest in capacity, they are creating a positively reinforcing cycle of change. They "manage up" and buffer the school from outside pressure to produce immediate results so that there is space for educators to focus on building the capacity needed for longer-term change.

Coherence

- Effective leadership for strategic improvement includes an understanding of how culture, resources, and structures are deeply connected and intertwined. It recognizes that pulling on one of these elements will impact the others.
- Leaders see how their actions need to be coherent with the culture they want to create. To facilitate trust, they need to be consistent in their actions and act in a trustworthy manner.
- Policies and structures that leaders uphold need to be in keeping with the goals of the organization. If they incent alternative behaviors, either the policy or structure needs to be changed.

References

Coyle, D. (2018). *The culture code: The secrets of highly successful groups.* New York, NY: Bantam.

DiAngelo, R. (2018). *White fragility: Why it's so hard for white people to talk about racism.* Boston, MA: Beacon Press.

Edmondson, A. C. (2002). *Managing the risk of learning: Psychological safety in work teams* (pp. 255–275). Cambridge, MA: Division of Research, Harvard Business School.

Edmondson, A. C. (2018). *The fearless organization: Creating psychological safety in the workplace for learning, innovation, and growth.* Hoboken, NJ: John Wiley & Sons.

Edmondson, A., & Verdin, P. (2017, November 13). *Your strategy should be a hypothesis you constantly adjust.* Retrieved May 26, 2020, from https://hbr.org/2017/11/your-strategy-should-be-a-hypothesis-you-constantly-adjust

Elmore, R. F. (2005). Accountable leadership. *The Educational Forum*, *69*(2), 134–142.

English, F. W. (2000). *Deciding what to teach and test: Developing, aligning, and auditing the curriculum*. Thousand Oaks, CA: Corwin Press

Kegan, R., & Lahey, L. L. (2016). *An everyone culture: Becoming a deliberately developmental organization*. Cambridge, MA: Harvard Business Review Press.

Kendi, I. X. (2019). *How to be an Antiracist*. New York, NY: One World/Ballantine.

Marshall, J. C. (2016). *The highly effective teacher: 7 classroom-tested practices that foster student success*. Alexandria, VA: ASCD.

Mehta, J., & Fine, S. (2015). Bringing values back in: How purposes shape practices in coherent school designs. *Journal of Educational Change*, *16*(4), 483–510.

Pollock, M. (2008). *Everyday antiracism: Getting real about race in schools*. New York, NY: New Press.

Schein, E. H. (2004). *Organizational culture and leadership* (3rd ed.). San Francisco, CA: Jossey-Bass.

Singleton, G. E. (2014). *Courageous conversations about race: A field guide for achieving equity in schools*. Thousand Oaks, CA: Corwin Press.

Skrla, L., McKenzie, K. B., & Scheurich, J. J. (Eds.). (2009). *Using equity audits to create equitable and excellent schools*. Thousand Oaks, CA: Corwin Press.

5 | Shared Understanding of High-Quality Teaching and Learning

Vignette: A Need for a Common Understanding of High-Quality Instruction

Once Ashburn developed their portrait of the graduate and their initial steps toward reaching their goals, Maria began working directly with the principals on enhancing instruction. She wanted to generate a concept of classroom instruction that included the experiences all students would need to develop the attributes described in the portrait.

She went into this process worried principals would resist giving up their school-based ideas of good instruction, but she was pleasantly surprised. It turned out the principals were quite relieved by the opportunity to collaborate on a district definition of high-quality instruction—they understood very quickly the benefits of a district-level approach. There were two reasons for this.

First, the principals considered it useful to be able to say to teachers, "We are doing this as a district." The message could now be reinforced in other schools, where many of the teachers had friends and often compared notes about practice. Indeed, in the current district culture, a principal or leadership team that wanted to promote instructional change in their school had to be willing to field questions from their staff about why they were expected to do work other teachers in the district were not—or, conversely, why another school's teachers received training or support unavailable to them.

Second, because there was no unifying definition of high-quality instruction in the district, when schools had to figure out what instructional improvements to use or support, it put a lot of extra work on the school. Often, each school had to independently reinvent the wheel regarding "good" instruction, attend new trainings, and build or adopt new lesson plans, materials, and assessments for each intervention they selected. Alternatively, a shared definition could help all the schools work together. Selections and the subsequent trainings and materials could be shared across schools and fully supported by central office staff.

It wasn't just the district that didn't have a shared understanding of high-quality instruction; the principals too were divided on the subject. Sometimes this difference showed up in the labels they used to describe good instruction (differentiation, cooperative learning, student discourse, etc.). Other times, differences were revealed through how they talked about classrooms district leaders observed; although two principals might both say that their schools were working on "student-centered learning," in practice their classrooms could look quite different.

Maria realized that, in addition to promoting a shared definition of good instruction, having a deep conversation about equity and how it showed up in daily instructional practices was also going to have to be a priority. While the old and new vision statements referred to "all students," it wasn't obvious to anyone how that was actually going to be achieved when the data showed disparities in outcomes for different groups of students by race and other demographic features. There was also little (if any) discussion about how current policies and structures might be contributing to these inequitable opportunities and outcomes and thus would need to be changed.

Maria began to plan for administrator meetings that would surface their mental models about what good instruction looked like and for whom. She believed such discussions would help them agree on the key components of powerful learning, analyze how well current practices were meeting these components, and build their capacity to lead the work of improving instruction across the district.

Chapter Overview

The purpose of this chapter is to give you a clear idea of what we mean by a shared understanding of high-quality instruction, also known as an instructional model, and why it's important. The chapter builds on the argument we have made in prior chapters: that a school district should have a cogent and coherent strategy for educational improvement that doesn't vary a great deal from school to school. We talk about why we think it's so crucial that everyone in a district be working with the same model for good instruction, what such a model should include, and how a shared understanding of high-quality instruction might be generated for the greatest benefit. By the end of the chapter, we hope you are convinced that having a shared instructional model is key to a strategy for continuous improvement and that you will have a good idea about how to create one, if it doesn't already exist in your district.

What Do We Mean by a Shared Understanding of High-Quality Instruction?

If you were to visit the local public school in your part of the country and observe half a dozen classrooms at random, what do you think you would find? The evidence suggests you would see a plethora of instructional practices in use. You might expect to find the greatest variation in a high school, where it's possible to see both "traditional" pedagogy—the teacher doing most of the talking, students taking notes, followed by a quiz on the material every few weeks—and more "progressive" approaches—lively classrooms with students working in groups to solve design challenges, such as creating an effective solar oven or considering how to represent the three branches of government in a compelling infographic. Moreover, this variety would be apparent across the schools in the district.

Likewise, if you were to ask a random assortment of teachers about the district's instructional focus, the responses could vary broadly. It's possible that you could hear a consistent, cogent explanation of the district strategy for improving outcomes for students, just as you could be met with shrugs and puzzled looks. The most likely response would be a list of initiatives launched somewhere in the district over the last several years and perhaps a commentary as to which of these were complete nonstarters, which could have been good if handled better, and which were abandoned too soon.

One of the most important factors in ensuring an effective strategy for improving outcomes for students is probably the most obvious, yet is also terribly neglected: everyone involved in instruction in the district has a shared understanding of what high-quality teaching and learning should be.

Underlying the power of an instructional model is the critical assumption that it will, when enacted fully, bring about improvements in learning opportunities and outcomes for students while simultaneously helping to accelerate the gains for those most marginalized in the current system. We construe a shared understanding of high-quality instruction to mean that there is agreement among the teachers, leaders, and other key staff in a district regarding what good teaching looks like, such that they know what they should see when they walk into a classroom and can distinguish between instruction that's aligned with the district's model and that which is not.

In our opinion, everyone involved in daily instruction must know:

- The district's stance on high-quality teaching and learning, why it was adopted, and what it means for the way educators do their work.
- The district's strategy and connected components for reaching the desired outcomes for all students according to their unique needs.
- How the components of the strategy fit together to support and reinforce each other.

As John Hattie (2012) pointed out, the job of educators is not necessarily to find out which instructional practices work generally, but rather what works best for their students in their context. Indeed, we have evidence that almost every instructional practice or intervention shows a positive impact on the students. However, these positive impacts are not evenly distributed. Some instructional approaches work better than others across contexts. Such differences have implications for both the degree of enhancements to student opportunity and outcomes and for the resources needed to produce these gains. These realities create the need to make trade-offs between resources and impact—for example, if the resource cost is quite high for an intervention and there is an alternative with slightly smaller effect sizes but much lower costs, the alternative might be a better choice. Alternatively, some interventions may not produce a very large effect size but are worth doing because the cost of implementation is low and its implementation will not preclude other changes with higher effect sizes being implemented (Wiliam, 2018).

While so far in this chapter we have advocated for a greater degree of consistency in districts' instructional approaches, we don't make the claim that all variation will or should be removed. Rather, we suggest such variation should be coherent and created by schools and the district together. The district's vision for high-quality instruction should allow for, when needed, deliberate and intentional grade-level or subject variation in implementation. For example, a decision may be made to teach a specific subject in a specific way because the subject demands it or because the developmental needs of some students differ from others (for example, kindergartners vs. high school juniors, students with developmental delays, etc.). This amounts to strategy maps and/or plans being *nested*—like *matryoshka*, they may vary in surface features and in scale, but they are very clearly related to each other, and fit inside one another perfectly.

Further, we neither advocate for a lock-step or scripted approach to teaching, nor do we think that teaching could ever become "teacher-proof." Quite the opposite. We see teaching as *the most* complex of human endeavors and therefore not reducible to a checklist or a rubric. Just because high-quality instruction is defined doesn't mean there won't be space for innovation or improvisation. In fact, having a stronger definition of what "good" looks like will likely elevate stronger instruction that leads to deeper learning, as opposed to unyielding alignment with a pacing guide. Teaching is so difficult that no one can ever do it perfectly, so the best chance there is of making the biggest difference for students is to constantly learn to teach better. We believe the best hope of doing this is for all the educators in a district to start with approaches already known to be effective and work collaboratively to improve them over time.

Why Should a District Adopt a Districtwide Vision of High-Quality Instruction?

Since teaching and learning is the core work of education, it follows that the key part of a strategy for improvement must encompass instruction. In other words, the district strategy should be anchored by a shared approach to instruction that doesn't vary a great deal from school to school.

We advocate that districts work toward implementing a districtwide model for high-quality instruction for the following reasons:

1. Some educational practices are higher leverage than others, and districts should take seriously their obligation to ensure teachers employ, and supervisors enable and reinforce, practices most likely to cause the largest gains for students.

2. As equity should be at the center of the district's vision and mission, there must be a clear standard of what high-quality instruction looks like, along with systems in place to ensure every classroom meets that standard, and direct and immediate interventions deployed when they do not.

3. There's a limit to the depth and breadth of practices a district can effectively support. If all teachers are expected to figure out for themselves which techniques are best, there's a diminished likelihood that the district can fully support these efforts, creating huge costs to efficiency and effectiveness.

4. A shared definition of high-quality instruction means more opportunities for teacher collaboration. Teachers adopting new practices go through a great deal of trial and error, leading to what Fullan (2001) labels an implementation dip. When educators collaborate to implement a practice, they can share their results, and therefore learn from each other's experience (Kruse et al., 1994; Weiner, 2014; Wiliam, 2007), thereby increasing learning and shortening the implementation dip.

5. Absent a shared focus for improvement, and given a teacher evaluation document that's intended to be comprehensive, evaluators must decide for themselves what to focus on when they evaluate teachers. Since evaluators all bring their own mental model of what good instruction looks like to their work, how teachers qualify for a high ranking in the evaluation system will vary according to the evaluator. This is fundamentally unfair and confusing to teachers. It's especially problematic in high schools, where it's not unheard of for teachers to be assigned a different evaluator several years in a row, with each one telling them something slightly different about how to improve their teaching.

There has been a gradual shift over the last 30 years from teachers operating separately from each other and making their own decisions about how to teach to much more collaborative, interdependent working conditions and clearer expectations for what will be taught. This has been fueled by research showing that collaboration among teachers is a key indicator of increased student learning (Ronfeldt et al., 2015).

We are bolstered by such findings. However, it's worth stating that while some collaboration may be better than no collaboration at all, collaboration around evidence-based instructional expertise is far better. Indeed, in our experience, when collaboration is present but good information is not, expertise and resource-seeking behaviors help to ensure teachers can leverage collaboration to create continuous improvement. These efforts become even more likely to succeed when the recent research (Johnson et al., 2014) indicates that a district creates an instructional model and infrastructure to support it.

What Should a District Stance on High-Quality Instruction Include?

High-Leverage Instructional Practices

A definition of high-quality instruction should be narrowly focused on the high-leverage practices deemed to create the greatest student learning based on resource availability. This definition should be distinct from teacher evaluation criteria as its purpose is different. Descriptions of instruction embodied in teacher evaluation rubrics are deliberately broad, covering all aspects of instruction to which the district must hold teachers accountable. School districts can and should articulate an instructional focus, beyond teacher evaluation, that represents the practices the district believes will have the greatest impact on improving student learning aligned with the portrait of the graduate.

Equity, too, is a key consideration in designing a definition of high-quality instruction. Throughout this book we have defined equity in terms of the opportunities, experiences, and outcomes that all students should enjoy, and the district stance on instruction should reinforce these elements. In making decisions about what instructional practices to focus on, districts should pay attention to the research on which practices promote opportunity, access, and high achievement for all students and include curricula that reflect students' experiences, high expectations from teachers (Weinstein, 2004), embedded formative assessment (Wiliam, 2011), and effective feedback (Hattie & Timperley, 2007). As we discuss in more detail in Chapter 6, a monitoring system that investigates whether tactics for increasing equity have the intended effects also needs to be part of the plan. Differentiation, for example, while admirable in theory, frequently manifests as students who are having difficulty being given far less challenging tasks than their higher achieving peers.

Curriculum

The idea that the curriculum should be designed backward from the goals for student achievement is not a new idea and is very similar in principle to our concept of strategy design. Still, we know from our experience and from research that students experience curricula that frequently fall short both in terms of a given year and in providing a coherent and scaffolded learning experience over time. In designing curricula to reach the district's strategic vision, the designers must make sure that there is a written curriculum, that it is aligned across grade levels, that it is both rigorous and scaffolded, and that engaging with it will result in students acquiring the knowledge, skills, and other characteristics included in the portrait of the graduate.

In addition to the structure of the written curriculum, equity plays a role here too. The curriculum should reflect the breadth and depth of society; all students should see themselves reflected in what their educational institutions determine is worth learning about. Another challenge is to ensure the curriculum is accelerated for students whose knowledge and skills are not yet aligned with standards, when frequently it is slowed down. Acceleration is often associated with high-achieving students, but students who did not receive the same opportunities or are lagging behind need it more.

Generating a Districtwide Shared Understanding of High-Quality Instruction

When we left the educators at Ashburn at the beginning of this chapter, they were just about to embark on creating a district instructional model, including agreeing on what matters most, reading relevant research, and building the instructional leadership skills of the administrators. We have worked with many districts on creating such a model. Often, this work takes much longer than they think it will, as they begin to realize they may have been using the same terminology (often based on the district's teacher evaluation instrument) to describe very different things. Or, they realize their expectations for the appropriate level of work for a certain grade level or group of students vary. The time this takes and the level of hidden disagreement it exposes sometimes come as a shock to participants, and this is especially true if the leaders began the process thinking or conveying the message that creating this shared definition would look like the half-day calibration training typical for many teacher evaluation instruments.

We find we can predict the range of responses we will get from showing a few videos of instruction we've found to generate the most discussion.

For example, there is a fourth grade lesson on electrical circuits that is a stellar example of direct instruction. Some viewers like the teaching because it is well organized, the students are well-behaved, the concepts are high level, the pace is good, and the students are on task. Some viewers find it underwhelming because it is so teacher-directed and the students are not being asked to generate questions or grapple with big ideas for themselves. The variation in opinion generated when a group of educators view the video provides fodder for healthy discussion which pushes the group closer to deciding what really matters.

In another example, there is a high school English class focused on character study. In this case, viewers like it because the teacher clearly has routines in place for modeling how she thinks, for having the students work collaboratively, and for checking in with multiple students to assess their progress. Frequently, however, the high school educators in the room are taken aback when the elementary folks say "10th grade? Are you sure? Because we have fourth graders doing this exact same thing."

The point here is that *despite* the commonality of a rubric for teacher evaluation or a published instructional framework or shared language to describe instruction (or maybe *because* of them), educators are frequently misled to believe agreement exists about what the key descriptors of pedagogy mean for instructional practice. And until there is agreement about good instruction, conversations about how to improve instruction are impotent. So how do you come to a shared understanding of what is meant by high-quality instruction?

Creating a Shared Understanding of High Quality Instruction
Development Process

Step One: Surfacing Individual Mental Models About Instruction

   a. **Individually**: Draw a visual representation or model of what you consider to be good instruction. *This should not be a metaphor*—no houses, gardens, school buses, or families. It should identify the component parts of high-quality instruction and how they are connected to each other.

   b. **In small groups**: Discuss how your models compare with one another. What emerges as most important? Based on your discussion, draw a model on chart paper that represents the collective thinking of the group.

Step Two: Identify Big Ideas

   a. **Gallery walk**: Display the models. Take time to look carefully at them. What do you notice?

   b. **Whole group**: What themes did you observe? *Note to the facilitator: Don't allow "jargon"—hold everyone accountable to clarifying terminology such as "student engagement" and "rigor." Challenge participants to generate precise descriptions of what they are looking for.* What emerges as most important to the group?

   c. **Draft a model**: This is almost impossible to do in a large group. Delegate one or two people, or a small group, to generate a revised model based on the work done so far. This can be written or graphic, but we find that it is easier to show the connections among elements of the definition if there is at least some graphical element to the model— perhaps arrows to show intended outcomes, for example.

Step Three: Find Anchor Texts and Shared Language

   a. **Decide what key ideas or themes to pursue further**: Use anchor texts to identify terms and definitions to use, and to research further. (For example, a group that decides it wants to pursue critical thinking and deep students engagement might read Mehta and Fine's (2019) *In Search of Deeper Learning. Note to the facilitator: Who decides what texts to read should be decided in advance.*

Step Four: Observe and Discuss Instruction

   a. Observe instruction: Visit classrooms or watch videos of teaching. Choose teaching to watch that is likely to provoke disagreement—resist the impulse to assume that using the same language denotes shared understanding. Maintain an equity lens—pay attention to any variation in students' experience traceable to race, gender, or other innate characteristic.

Step Five: Create a "Finalish" Draft of High-quality Instruction

   a. **Refine the model**. It should represent the best thinking of the group, but need not look polished or professional.

Step Six: Take the Show on the Road

   a. Create opportunities for all teachers and leaders to engage with the model. The goal is for them to make meaning of it, to discuss what it might look like at their grade level or in their subject, and to give input into what they might need in order to teach in line with the model.

Connecticut Center for School Change. Used with permission.

Figure 5.1 Creating a Shared Understanding of HQI

We've come up with six steps to create such an understanding based on our work with different groups, as seen in Figure 5.1. We provide a process for the steps and also discuss them here to provide more context—note that we refer to this as a process rather than a protocol, as the steps described may be spread out over weeks or months.

We recommend you go through these steps first as you develop your proposed activities around instruction via the backward mapping activity (see Chapter 3) during the early stages of implementation, and then later, when you have data to assess them, consider whether and to what degree performance issues may be linked to differences in understanding of high-quality instruction. Remember, too, that the deeper your implementation goes, the more nuanced your understanding will be. And the more nuanced the understandings are, the more you will inevitably be pushed toward a need for further discussion and understanding about instructional practice.

For example, returning to Ashburn's plan, one of the instructional goals was to enhance teachers' ability to provide challenging tasks for all students. At the onset, what teachers believe regarding students' abilities may be limited and hence what they see as a challenge incomplete. However, as they engage in the work and grow in their skills and expectations, they may come to see how what they initially thought was rigor or a challenge might need to be modified. They may also learn to see and understand subtle differences in how students respond to challenges and modify their instructional practice in similarly subtle ways. This underscores the need for conversations about the meaning and manifestation of high-quality instruction to be ongoing. To push the district toward more tightly aligned classroom practices, the steps below should be used across all stages of the plan.

Last, and just to be clear, we list these steps as though they are totally discrete, but conversation happens at multiple points in this process. For example, as stated in Step One, it really helps to have a partner to talk through your mental model with who will ask you lots of clarifying questions, with the assumption they are there just to help you think through what is important, rather than correcting your mistaken ideas.

Step One: Surfacing Individual Mental Models About Instruction

It's difficult to share your mental model if you're unclear about what it is yourself. So, the first step is to ask educators to describe what they would hope to see in a classroom visit.

The graphics that educators draw frequently need additional explanation, so we give people time to talk to one another about what they have drawn and to ask questions. We worked with a superintendent who was adamant that students should not be seated in rows. It took quite a lot of probing for the superintendent to be able to articulate what rows represented to her and what was so special about sitting in groups. From this conversation we learned that what really mattered to her was that students learn to collaborate with one another on real-world problems, that they have agency in what they work on and how they work on it, that they know how to give and receive feedback, that they support one another, that they share responsibility for the outcome and for the learning, that they can monitor their own learning, that they can make their thinking visible through words and pictures—and more.

It became clear that the seating arrangement, while probably necessary for the kind of experience she wanted students to have, was actually a proxy for her ideal classroom. Obviously, there's a big difference between that description of what a classroom should look like and "I don't want to see any more rows!" but unless she was really explicit about everything she wanted to see and not just the classroom configuration, she was causing confusion in her staff.

This example illustrates a common problem. Just like this superintendent's focus on students working in groups when really she meant a lot more than that, definitive statements regarding "do's and don'ts" of instruction often function as intellectual shortcuts that assume a shared understanding that may not exist. The initial mental models that educators draw or describe tend to include several intellectual shortcuts, and so we have to dig deeper and ask questions such as:

1. What do you mean by that?
2. What would you expect to see students doing?

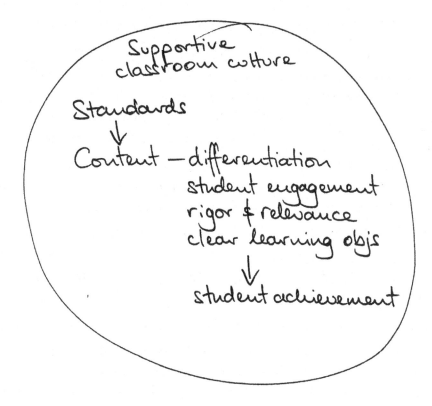

Figure 5.2 Maria's First Attempt

3. Why is it important?

4. What is the result you're looking for?

Figure 5.2 shows the preliminary model superintendent Maria created for what she thought high-quality instruction should like in Ashburn. What do you notice? Do you see any relationship between it and the final map?

Step Two: Identify Big Ideas

Once everyone has shared and perhaps clarified and refined their vision for what good instruction looks like, the group should take some time to review the graphics and look for themes. Again, this tends to produce a list of constructs at a high level of generality, such as differentiation, personalized learning, student-centered learning, relationships, feedback, engagement, rigor, student voice and choice, project-based learning, student agency, group work, student discourse, etc. It helps to collectively try to sort out what is meant by each of these terms.

Another way to reach clarity about what good instruction looks like is to take what participants in this exercise generate and ask questions that invite elaboration, such as:

1.   What does this mean for what the teacher should be doing?
2.   What does this mean for what the student should be doing?
3.   What does this mean for the kind of task the students should be working on?
4.   What does this mean for how classrooms should be structured?
5.   What does this mean for classroom routines?

And so on.

In Ashburn's case, questions about challenge might provoke conversations about what a challenging task looks like, as well as for whom and why. The responses could bring out some biased views of particular groups of students that would need to be attended to in the moment and then throughout the year as the work progressed. These questions might also provide opportunities for teachers to articulate some other convergent (and perhaps lots of divergent) ideas about challenging instruction, with lots of juicy conversation as those teaching different content at different levels weighed in. As this conversation evolved and participants talked about how they engage in these practices as well as what they know of the research, so too would we anticipate the map itself to evolve. For example, it may be the case that such a conversation leads schools to advocate for additional resources for coaching teachers on what challenging work is. Or they could build in more school-to-school or classroom-to-classroom visits to help ensure everyone has opportunities to consider challenge in contexts outside their own. Or, as we discuss next, there could be suggestions about research teachers should read and discuss on this topic.

Step Three: Find Anchor Texts and Shared Language

We advocate finding the time for serious, shared study of research-based texts. This is helpful for several reasons, most obviously because the practices you choose to implement in service of improved student achievement should have a positive track record of creating the changes you hope to see.

In addition, creating a canon of books and articles that everyone in the organization reads facilitates the work of creating a shared understanding of high-quality instruction because it provides clarity about the meaning of the terms you use as well as the terminology itself. Looking at multiple definitions of a term also illustrates how much variation in meaning there is in just one construct. For example, here are some definitions of engagement taken from several popular books over the last few years:

Marzano (2007a) refers to engagement as "students attending to the instructional activities occurring in class" (p. 99) and suggests that the following five areas can provide useful insights into how teachers might increase student engagement:

- High energy
- Missing information
- The self-system
- Mild pressure
- Mild controversy and competition

Schlechty (2011, p. 14), on the other hand, suggests that "four components are always present when a student is engaged:

1. The engaged student is attentive, in the sense that he or she pays attention to and focuses on the tasks associated with the work being done.

2. The engaged student is committed. He or she voluntarily (that is, without the promise of extrinsic rewards or the threat of negative consequences) deploys scarce resources under his or her control (time, attention, and effort, for example) to support the activity called for the by task.

3. The engaged student is persistent. He or she sticks with the task even when it presents difficulties.

4. The engaged student finds meaning and value in the tasks that make up the work."

Fredricks (2014) suggests that true engagement combines several components: behavioral (well-behaved and on-task), emotional (caring about the task or the subject), and cognitive (students thinking deeply, critically, and expansively about the task or subject). It's possible for students to be engaged in one component without being engaged in the others.

Providing varying definitions to groups meets several ends, including helping them see that many terms have multiple meanings, and, through discussion, helping them to move closer to a shared understanding of the term. We could understand, in the context of Ashburn, how differing research about how various conceptualizations of challenge (as well as what is considered challenging and for whom, and how it might be implemented) could evoke quite fiery and useful debates that could push not just understanding of these concepts but also cultural norms of professional debate and collaboration grounded in research use—an experience that may be new for some educators.

Considering the potentially provocative nature of this step, you can imagine the need for mezzanine leaders (see Chapter 4 for a full description of this position) and collaborative structures (professional learning communities, communities of practice, etc.) to be deployed to help teachers engage in the work.

Step Four: Watch Instruction and Talk About What You See

As described above, it's important to give educators the opportunity to examine whether the language they've debated and the diagrams they've created hold up to scrutiny. The best way to do that is to watch instruction and see if the observers have the same reactions. What does it mean if some think the teacher's questions are excellent and others think that the teacher is asking too many questions? What should happen if some observers think the teacher is doing a great job of encouraging productive struggle and others think that it's a mistake not to step in and correct misconceptions? How are you going to resolve the tension between observers who think that the students are engaged if they're on task and those who think that engagement has more to do with the cognitive work that the task demands of the students?

We have seen this work done in several different ways. In one district, the superintendent organized classroom visits over several years using the Instructional Rounds process, with a highly scripted routine to push the group to reach consensus on the features of good instruction, to assess whether that was actually what they were seeing in classrooms, and decide what capacity building needed to happen in order to move instruction closer to the district definition of high quality. In another district, the superintendent devoted most of the time during administrator gatherings to watching videos and asking the observers to make judgments and come to agreement about the quality of what they saw. In a third district, the superintendent made a major investment in bringing teachers and leaders from all schools in the district together for a week in the summer to watch the same instruction, combining the debrief of the observation with workshops intended to refine their shared understanding of high-quality instruction and also expand their capacity to support its development in their schools.

Disagreement is uncomfortable. It is tempting to give in to the desire to avoid conflict by allowing tacit assumptions to go unchallenged—for example, by deciding not to question whether everyone means the same thing by "engagement," or that "teacher talk" is a bad thing (we're not saying it's a good thing, just that you should be clear about what you think is important, and why).

Maintaining an equity lens is also important here. If the teacher is calling only on students who raise their hands (a questionable practice in itself), who is being called on, especially when the question is more challenging? If the teacher is "differentiating instruction," what does that mean for the level of rigor of the task students are set? Whom does the teacher praise? Whom does the teacher discipline or redirect? Does the teacher respond differently to girls versus boys?

Step Five: Create a "Finalish" Draft Definition of High-Quality Instruction

This is very messy work, and there is a strong temptation to make it look less messy—to turn the handwritten diagram into a fancy PowerPoint slide

or colorful infographic. Just be aware that when you do that, its funda-
mental nature has changed. It stops being an imperfect attempt to capture
everyone's best thinking about good instruction and starts being immutable
and therefore impervious to feedback. We advocate leaving the model in
draft form for as long as possible, so that as many people as possible get to
engage with it and so that it's easier to change as other parts of the strategy
are built out and make it necessary to change the draft model.

We see the definition of high-quality instruction as both a stand-alone
document and a key component of other resources. For example, teachers
should be able to find the instructional model easily on the district website,
and curriculum documents should refer to it. Also, the instructional model
is a part of the strategy—it is, in fact, an elaborated version of the column
of the strategy map that describes what teachers will do to ensure students
reach the portrait of the graduate. And it is, for districts that have a Response
to Intervention plan (also known as a multitiered system of support), tier
one of that plan. It is also the basis for the district's teacher evaluation plan.

We think you should spend time representing it graphically, but not as
a branding exercise or a communication device. We believe strongly that
if teachers are going to be expected to teach as the instructional model
requires, they will need the time and the opportunity to make meaning of
it, so they develop a rounded understanding of what it should look like not
in the abstract, but in their own classrooms. It will not and cannot include
every school- and teacher-level difference in terms of their needs and
approach or it will become impossibly difficult to use. But that's why it's so
important that every teacher be afforded the opportunity to explore what it
will look like in *their* classroom. It's a guiding document, with schools differentiating their specific approach based on context and need. Figure 5.3
represents Superintendent Jenkins' district's graphic looked like at the end
of this process—compare it with Maria's own first attempt (Figure 5.2).

Step Six: Take the Show on the Road

We find there's an assumption that once one group has created a definition
of high-quality instruction, the definition can be shared with others without
any loss of meaning. This turns out not to be the case. Everyone needs the
opportunity to process and construct understanding, so it's important that

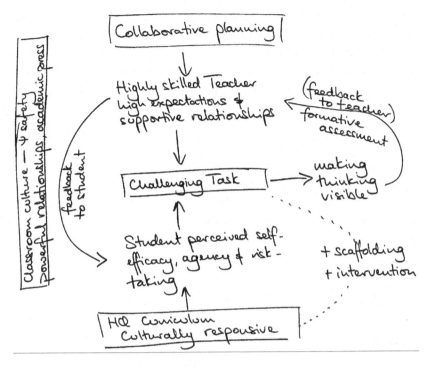

Figure 5.3 Ashburn's Working Model

both time and opportunity are provided for that to happen within the larger district community.

When we suggest multiple groups be afforded the chance to make collective sense of what is meant by high-quality instruction, we are often met with the concern that this will become unwieldy; that there will be multiple definitions in play. Admittedly, it can be challenging to keep track of who was involved at what stage of the process, especially in a large district, but it's worth figuring out. And there's no reason why each group must work in isolation, not knowing what other groups have done. Some districts make good use of a shared file service like Google Drive to make the work of all groups available to everyone. Some include time for a group like an elementary school faculty to synthesize their thinking with work done at another school. Some charge a group like a curriculum council or all the district subject coordinators with the responsibility of taking the input from all the groups and creating a formal definition. Some start with a kind of guiding coalition charged with going out to schools to elicit feedback on a first draft. All of these are valid approaches, as is any other that fully involves the community in meaning making around these issues.

The goal is to generate shared understanding, so that teachers know what to aim for in planning instruction, and not to require a supervisor to tell them what "good" looks like. We find it ironic that there is so much discussion about providing learning objectives and success criteria for each lesson because of the benefit to students, and yet the only time some teachers are involved in discussions about success criteria for their own work is at the end-of-year evaluation conference.

With that said, and as we discuss further in Chapter 6, there should be routines built into the plan that ensure that the conversation regarding high-quality instruction is ongoing at all levels of the system, and that these conversations are grounded in data to support continual improvement over time.

Return to Principles

Equity

- Just as the vision of the school district must clearly apply to all students, the district's definition of high-quality instruction must mean that all students experience appropriately challenging and supportive curriculum and instruction.

- The curriculum should be culturally inclusive and free from stereotyping of and bias toward race, gender, religion, and so on.

Logic

- It should be clear how the district's definition of high-quality instruction is the mechanism for reaching the portrait of the graduate.

- The end result of the definition of high-quality instruction should be the attainment of the portrait of the graduate.

Capacity

- A lot is riding on the ability of educators to deliver the instructional system that is the backbone of the district strategy. Building the capacity of educators to do that is essential to the success of the strategy.

Coherence

- When the district identifies the instructional system that it believes will result in students reaching the portrait of the graduate, all the planning for the work of the rest of the district must be aligned to the work of the instructional system. This is how the district becomes coherent.

References

Fredricks, J. A. (2014). *The eight myths of student disengagement: Creating classrooms of deep learning.* Thousand Oaks, CA: Corwin Press.

Fullan, M. (2001). *Leading in a culture of change.* San Francisco: Jossey-Bass.

Hattie, J. (2012). *Visible learning for teachers: Maximizing impact on learning.* New York, NY: Routledge.

Hattie, J., & Timperley, H. (2007). The power of feedback. *Review of Educational Research, 77*(1), 81–112.

Johnson, S. M., Marietta, G., Higgins, M. C., Mapp, K. L., & Grossman, A. S. (2014). *Achieving coherence in district improvement: Managing the relationship between the central office and schools.* Cambridge, MA: Harvard Education Press.

Kruse, S., Louis, K. S., & Bryk, A. (1994). Building professional community in schools. *Issues in Restructuring Schools, 6*(3), 67–71.

Marzano, R. J. (2007a). *The art and science of teaching: A comprehensive framework for effective instruction.* Alexandria, VA: ASCD. pp. 99–100.

Marzano, R. (2007b). Designing a comprehensive approach to classroom assessment. In D. Reeves (Ed.), *Ahead of the curve: The power of assessment to transform teaching and learning.* Bloomington, IN: Solution Tree.

Mehta, J., & Fine, S. (2019). *In search of deeper learning: The quest to remake the American high school.* Cambridge, MA: Harvard University Press.

Ronfeldt, M., Farmer, S. O., McQueen, K., & Grissom, J. A. (2015). Teacher collaboration in instructional teams and student achievement. *American Educational Research Journal, 52*(3), 475–514.

Schlechty, P. C. (2011). *Engaging students: The next level of working on the work.* San Francisco, CA: Jossey-Bass.

Weiner, J. M. (2014). Disabling conditions: Investigating instructional leadership teams in action. *Journal of Educational Change, 15*(3), 253–280.

Weinstein, R. S. (2004). *Reaching higher: The power of expectations in schooling.* Cambridge, MA: Harvard University Press.

Wiliam, D. (2007). Changing classroom practice. *Educational Leadership, 65*(4), 36–42.

Wiliam, D. (2011). *Embedded formative assessment.* Bloomington, IN: Solution Tree Press.

Wiliam, D. (2018). *Creating the schools our children need: Why what we're doing now won't help much (and what we can do instead).* West Palm Beach, FL: Learning Sciences International.

PART 3

Monitoring and Continuous Improvement

6 | How Do We Know It Is Working?

Vignette: Developing Routines

Maria understood that a plan that simply takes up space on a shelf does nothing to drive the work of improvement. Hence, she was very deliberate in setting up routines that demanded using information about how the plan was being implemented. This information would be used to drive conversations about whether implementation was going as planned and whether the strategy was getting the anticipated results. For example, one of the routines she put in place was regular visits to classrooms to see one aspect of the plan in operation: formative assessment.

During a visit to the comprehensive high school, small groups made up of administrators and teachers from across the district fanned out across the school to see classrooms in action with a particular question in mind: are teachers eliciting evidence of student understanding during instruction and using that evidence to make in-the-moment instructional decisions? At the allotted time, they reconvened in the library.

In the conversation that followed, the small groups debriefed what they had seen, and then Maria facilitated a whole-group conversation. The takeaways included:

- There was considerable variation in practice from classroom to classroom. In one classroom they saw no evidence of formative assessment embedded in the teaching; instead, the teacher was focused solely on whether the answer he solicited was correct.

In another classroom, they saw instruction engineered so that students understood what they were trying to achieve, could assess their own performance, and got feedback from the teacher and their peers.

- There was disagreement among the observers as to whether what they saw constituted formative assessment and whether the formative assessment was purposeful.

Based on these takeaways, the group made some recommendations for next steps. Clearly, some teachers had a good handle on formative assessment and were implementing it successfully. But it appeared others did not. The group recommended some differentiation in the professional development offered to teachers and some intentional deployment of instructional coaching. Additionally, and given the disagreement among the observers about quality formative assessment practices, the group recommended that they collaborate in collecting resources, reading research, and meeting again to see if they could move closer to a shared understanding of what high-quality formative assessment should look like. They believed such efforts could help them be better leaders of these efforts and better support implementation in their schools.

Chapter Overview

In this chapter we focus on the final row, and a critical element, of an effective Disciplined Strategic Plan: monitoring and accountability. A major part of a leader's role is to ensure that routines are put in place to collect data about the implementation of the strategy—data that can then be used to evaluate how well the strategy is working and what can be done to improve it. We start with the assumption that the business of education is large and complex, and there are no foolproof prescriptions for what initiatives, programs, or actions will lead inexorably to all students developing the traits in the portrait of the graduate.

Figuring out what can be measured along the way to make sure the strategy is being enacted as planned or whether it needs to be adjusted is one of the most challenging parts of planning. In our experience, educators resist having the discussion about measuring implementation because it is complicated and often enmeshed with other areas of the district's work, especially evaluating teachers and leaders, which can include difficult conversations. However, being able to monitor the implementation of a strategy is essential to its success. How else will you be able to predict whether you're going to reach your desired outcomes or know what adjustments to your plan you need to make?

To start, we talk about accountability in the context of strategic planning in an effort to help shift thinking toward a more positive and formative approach. Next, we highlight what specifically we want to measure to help ensure we're gathering the right information to make the best decisions regarding the progression of the plan. We close with a discussion of how, once you know why and what you are measuring, it's important to create routines that move you toward a state of constant growth and improvement and allow you to weather the rapidly changing needs of teachers and students in an ever-shifting environment.

Rethinking Accountability

When we talk to educators about the concept of accountability—specifically, how to hold educators accountable to ensure strategic efforts are moving in the right direction—we're often met with looks of resignation. As we discuss these issues further, it often comes out that they have come to conflate accountability with high-stakes accountability—a prevailing policy of inspection, standardized tests, and external pressures to meet unrealistic outcomes with limited resources. This is not the accountability we're referring to. Like many tools, accountability can be used in lots of ways and to many ends. We hope to show you that accountability doesn't need to be negative or top-down. Rather, it can help you create meaningful signposts toward your strategic goals, drive better decisions, and celebrate success.

As we discussed earlier in the book, because of the accountability movement, educators are used to thinking of accountability as attached to individuals, as in "we have to hold them accountable." The basic assumption often driving current policies of accountability seems to be that people require constant watching to ensure they effectively and efficiently engage in their work. By this way of thinking, people only do what you want them to do if you check up on them and make sure they're doing it: "what gets measured gets done." There are a number of problems with this approach that we think are worth naming and critiquing.

First, this view of human behavior ignores the simplest explanation for someone not doing what they are supposed to do—they don't know how to do it (or, we would add, don't have the supports necessary to do it in the way desired). This is Hanlon's Razor; whereas Occam's Razor says that if there are two competing theories, the simpler one is preferable, Hanlon's Razor says that you should not attribute to malice what can be explained through a lack of capacity (individual or organizational).

Second, it assumes people are motivated by measurement. To a certain extent, that is true. However, as we noted in Chapter 3, this is only part of the story. Performance goals are only useful if people know how meet those goals and have the tools to do so. Similarly, accountability doesn't create motivation; rather, it helps to tell us whether people have what they need to competently engage. As Elliot and Dweck (2005) highlight in their concept of competence motivation, people don't need external pushes to want to succeed. People are naturally motivated to attain competence, and the pursuit of competence can facilitate an orientation toward continued learning and growth (that is, a growth mindset). Moreover, people only feel competent when they receive the necessary support and infrastructure to meet the goals to which they are being held accountable. Elmore (2004) coined the phrase "reciprocal accountability" to describe the idea that we shouldn't be asking more of educators than we are willing to commit in resources to support them. In this framing of accountability, the focus becomes identifying how we can best build educators' competence and capacity. As such, our very reasons for engaging accountability shift from "catching" or punishing poor performers to identifying the supports (leadership actions and professional learning) educators need to reach the goals identified in the Disciplined Strategic Plan.

The third and final problem with the current approach to accountability is that it overemphasizes outcomes at the cost of ignoring processes and conditions or how we go about the business of learning and teaching. If anyone needs evidence of why a single-minded focus on outcomes might be problematic, we need look no further than the research showing how teachers have shifted their time and instruction to tested subjects at the cost of the arts, physical education, and other nontested areas in response to high-stakes testing (Dee et al., 2010; Hannaway & Hamilton, 2008). The Atlanta cheating scandal (Saultz et al., 2016) and the many others that were equally problematic but less publicized, gives us important insights into what happens when we emphasize outcomes over the work itself.

What we hope we have made clear is that we think the assumptions underlying current accountability systems are problematic and that by using different assumptions to guide our accountability practices, we can do so much better, and so much more. For us, and for the purpose of Disciplined Strategy Mapping, the assumptions driving accountability in this context should be:

1. When people don't perform, it's because they lack the skills, knowledge, or resources to do so.
2. People are motivated by believing they can meet the goals set by the organization and by a positive professional culture which values hard work and learning.
3. We need to measure processes and outcomes to facilitate improvement.

Given these assumptions, it's important that any accountability system used for Disciplined Strategic Planning is one that focuses on identifying:

*   Current and evolving levels of capacity over time (What resources are being provided? To what degree are these resources being utilized?)
*   Whether people (and educators) are growing and learning over time (Are teachers shifting in their knowledge, beliefs, skills, etc.?)
*   The degree the learning is changing practice and outcomes (Are teachers implementing the desired interventions? Are they positively impacting students' learning?)

With these needs and proposed questions in mind, we now shift to talk about some of the measures that might be useful to consider as you develop your plan.

Measures to Consider

To meet the above criteria of an accountability system for learning and gather data that facilitates a full picture of the implementation of your strategy, you'll need to know:

- Are resources being provided, and to what degree is this the case?
- Are educators, students, and any other mentioned participants in the plan fully utilizing the resources and doing so correctly?
- Are the infusion and implementation of the resources changing practice and outcomes?

As you might have noticed, the proposed measures include those pertaining not just to students or to educators, but to both (and any other plan participants for that matter). In the plans we have seen, all too often the focus is on students and how their work or test scores were affected. This focus treats the process between the conceptualization of the plan and enhanced student outcomes as a black box—failing to acknowledge the shifts in understanding, knowledge, and practice adults (and, most often, teachers) must go through for the plan to be successful. To create a learning organization, we must treat everyone as learners, engaging the same principles of formative assessment we so often use for students with educators.

To do so, while simultaneously ensuring we're covering all the parts of the learning process, we must focus on capturing Outputs and Outcomes for educators and students over time. See Table 6.1 for an overview of these concepts.

Outputs

Metaphorically, we might think about your district or school as a person striving to become healthier. The Disciplined Strategy Map is the treatment plan. In the case of Ashburn, for example, we might consider the efforts to provide professional support to teachers to enhance their instructional practice as one part of the treatments and students' access to classrooms that more fully embrace their multifaceted identities as another.

Table 6.1 Outputs vs. Outcomes

	Output	*Outcome*
Definition	Direct results of interventions toward capacity building aligned with Disciplined Strategic Plan.	Specific changes in beliefs, behaviors, and outcomes due to implementation of activities from Disciplined Strategic Plan.
Questions Answered about Intervention	Did it happen? How often? How many attended? What was discussed?	What was learned? Did it shift their practice? Are the outcomes better?
Potential Measurement Tools	Schedules Agendas Attendance rolls	Quality surveys Observations of practice Knowledge assessments

Outputs, then, are measures of whether the treatment made it to the patient as planned (did they get their dose?). In this way, outputs are the direct results of the treatment and are most often framed in terms of frequency, size, and scope. Aligned measures would be things like schedules, attendance rolls, and meeting agendas showing what specific topics were covered. Returning to the example from Ashburn, given their efforts to enhance teachers' instructional practice by providing ongoing support, we would want to assess whether this support was provided, how often, and if teachers showed up to these sessions. This may sound fairly rudimentary, but anyone who has attended professional development sessions, whether embedded in the school or provided externally, can attest to the fact that they often get cancelled or pushed off, happen less often than they should, and have lower attendance than expected.

Similarly, at a student level, we could imagine that as part of the initiative to enhance school culture, teachers at the middle school created an advisory block to explore students' identities and engage in activities related to social justice and activism. This would be the treatment. The degree to which teachers engaged the time in these ways and used the materials provided, as well as whether students came to these sessions and how fully they participated, would perhaps all be outputs of interest. The reason it's important to capture such information is that, just as it would be unlikely for a person to get better if they weren't given or didn't take medicine, so too would it be unlikely for the professional development to have the intended effect if it wasn't fully implemented or well attended. We wouldn't expect teachers to improve their practice if they didn't receive the associated support, and we wouldn't expect the culture to improve if students never truly engaged in the advisory sessions. And yet, it's often the case that educators implement such interventions without creating output measures to ensure they occur.

Alternatively, it's also the case that output measures are the only ones captured to assess an intervention. The problem with this approach is that while output measures tell us whether the treatment was delivered and in what dose, they don't tell us whether the treatment worked. In other words, outputs fail to provide us information about whether and to what degree anything changed because of implementation. To measure this change requires outcomes.

Outcomes

Outcomes are specific changes in beliefs, knowledge, behaviors, and impacts due to implementation of the activities from the Disciplined Strategic Plan. Outcomes facilitate our ability to move from "Did it happen?" to "What did it do?" and "How well did it do it?"

At the adult level, for example, and given that associated output measures confirmed that teachers indeed received support to enhance their practice, outcome measures in Ashburn might be focused on whether teachers had begun to think about their instruction differently or implement some of their new learning in their classrooms. We would also want to capture the degree to which these activities translated into enhanced student learning and achievement. It would be helpful too if these assessments were aligned with the measures to which educators and students will ultimately be held accountable.

Or, looking at the other intervention mentioned above and focused on the student advisories, we'd want to know if teachers had begun to talk about students in less deficit-oriented ways or seemed more inclined to tackle more difficult conversations of equity in their advisory sessions. Later, we could ask students how connected they felt to the school and whether the learnings from the advisory sessions were showing up in other courses or in greater opportunities for traditionally marginalized students to gain access to some of the higher-level courses. On this note, it's essential that any data collected regarding outcomes be carefully disaggregated. This would include breaking the data down by demographic variables (race, gender, special education identification, etc.) and potentially other factors of interest that might facilitate the identification of patterns of opportunity or performance. For example, it might be useful to disaggregate math performance data by how long the students have been enrolled at the school, by the feeder school they attended, or by the pattern of teachers they experienced. Each of these decisions would support a deeper understanding of the mechanisms that serve to produce differentiated opportunities and outcomes for different kids.

Clearly, there is a temporal quality to outcomes in that it is likely that specific changes in outcomes may occur at different times, with student outcomes lagging those of adults. For example, we might imagine it would be difficult for student outcomes to be dramatically enhanced before teachers are fully implementing a new strategy. There may also be a progression to the adult learning—perhaps teachers would need to change their beliefs before their practice, or vice versa. While it's less important which of these phenomena you think has to happen in what order, it is helpful to name these trajectories from the beginning and measure each phase of them. Doing so will allow you to better track your strategy and thus intervene and adjust as needed.

Which Assessments Tools to Choose?

Now that we've gone over why we're measuring and what types of measures we might use, when, and for whom, the next natural question is: what assessment tools should we use to collect this information? Given the broad array of tools most educators come into daily contact with (surveys, informal interviews, observations, standardized tests, exit tickets, etc.), the question is a reasonable one. However, just like when we provide in-person supports regarding the planning and accountability process to districts and school leaders, here we don't take a strong position on which specific tools

Strategy/Strategic Priority/Goal: Name of the project/strategy/focus area/goal		Theory of Action: them to monitor
A. What do Central Office leaders need to learn?	B. What do Central Office leaders need to do?	C. What do principals need to learn?
What knowledge, skills, and/or dispositions do central office leaders need to learn in order to support the system that supports the strategy? This description becomes the leadership development plan for Central Office leaders.	**What leadership actions are we expecting from central office leaders?** This description includes supervision of principals, to ensure that their leadership development needs are being met (Cell J) and that they are doing what is required of them (Cell K).	**What knowledge, skills, and/or dispositions do principals need to learn in order to provide professional learning for teachers (Cell E) and to create the conditions for instruction described in Cell F?** This description becomes the leadership development plan for building leaders.
H. How will we know?	I. How will we know?	J. How will we know?
How will we know that central office leaders have acquired these traits?	**How will we know that Central Office leaders are leading as intended?** Whose job is it to know and what are they going to do about it?	**How will we know that principals have acquired these traits?** Whose job is it to know, how will they know, and what are they going to do about it?

Figure 6.1 Annotated Strategy Map Template

The overarching logic behind the strategy, e.g. If all students receive feedback that causes their comprehension and take appropriate next steps, their achievement will increase.			
D. What do principals need to do?	E. What do teachers need to learn?	F. How will teachers teach?	G. What do we want for our students?
What leadership actions are we expecting from principals? To ensure that: a) teachers get the professional learning they need (Cell L, including training, coaching, and feedback; b) teachers get what they need to teach e.g. books and materials; c) The outcomes in Cells L, M, and N are monitored and discussed in supervision conversations; d) Adjustments are made in response to data.	**What knowledge, skills, and/or dispositions do teachers need to acquire in order to create the classroom experiences for students described in Cell F?** This description, in combination with what we know about how professionals learn most effectively, becomes the professional learning plan for the teachers implicated in the strategy.	**What instruction do we want students to experience that will lead to the intended outcomes for them?** Also known as the Instructional Model, Tier I instruction, or a model such as reading workshop, depending on the strategy. This instructional focus should be aligned to core documents in the district, including SRBI, teacher evaluation, and professional learning (see Cell E). How will teachers assess and respond to student learning?	**What knowledge, skills, and/or dispositions do we want students to acquire?** This will differ according to the mission of the school/district and the scale of the strategy. For example, a district improvement map may include here the Profile of the Graduate, and a literacy map may include specific decoding and comprehension skills.
K. How will we know?	L. How will we know?	M. How will we know?	N. How will we know?
How will we know that principals are leading as intended? Whose job is it to know, how will they know, and what are they going to do about it?	**How will we know that teachers have acquired these traits?** Whose job is it to know, and what are they going to do about it?	**How will we know that the instruction we want is taking place?** Who is going to observe in classrooms, how often, and what are they looking for?	**What metrics will we use to measure the outcomes?** Who is paying attention to these outcomes and how do they respond?

Figure 6.1 (Continued)

you should use to measure any or all of the elements of your plan. With that said, we do have some guidance on how you might go about selecting an assessment tool.

First, does the tool measure what you want to know? This point might feel relatively obvious, but given our experience of so many assessment tools used in schools feeling externally imposed and only remotely related to measuring what we really want to know about instruction or student performance, it's worthwhile to mention.

Any tool you select should help you better understand a specific question or group of questions related to the intervention. For example, if you wanted to know whether teachers were learning how to implement a new instructional technique—let's say reader's workshop—you might begin by asking the following questions:

- Do teachers know the key elements of reader's workshop?
- What's missing in their understanding?
- Do they feel ready to implement?

To see more about what such questions might look like across the Disciplined Strategy Map and how they link to specific interventions, see Figure 6.1.

These questions point to a need to hear from teachers directly about their experiences and knowledge, so we'd look for a tool that would help us get information about these elements. A really good tool might even give us granular enough information to allow us to differentiate our approach moving forward and support teachers based on their specific learning needs.

Using a teacher-centered tool that gets at learning is quite different than focusing on what students are doing or how well teachers are implementing. A tool for the former would likely require some kind of student-centered assessment, and the latter a tool that allows you to see the teacher in action. While either of these tools would give you interesting and potentially useful information, they wouldn't directly answer your questions and so aren't right for this specific part of the map.

This type of alignment between questions of interest and tools requires a somewhat narrower focus than perhaps we're used to regarding assessment, and also reemphasizes that student assessments are not really the right tool to get at teacher learning.

Now What? Making Accountability an Organizational Routine

Here we return to the purpose for all this measurement and accountability: to create meaningful signposts toward your goals, to drive you forward making better decisions, and to celebrate success. Achieving these purposes means not just collecting data, but doing something with it. Specifically, the data should be used to make regular decisions on whether to adjust, refine, double down on, or eliminate activities associated with your plan. To achieve this level of knowledge, you must understand the purpose of accountability and how to measure the things you care about. It also means that measurement and accountability practices become deeply embedded in your daily routines.

Without moving *all* the activities of the plan (including measurement) into the regular and daily practices of the school, it is unlikely to succeed. A plan doesn't govern people's day-to-day work; routines do. That's true of implementation of a plan and of using data to measure progress and to make adjustments to the plan and the overall strategy as a result. The key, then, to continuous improvement is to create routines that fulfill those needs.

Resnick and Spillane (2006) use the term "kernel routine" to denote an organizational routine that has the potential for transforming school practice. We can think of routines as falling into two types. There are the regular, boring routines of most organizations that are:

- Regularly occurring
- Predictable
- Utilize norms, tools, and protocols
- Embedded in the organizational culture ("this is the way we do things around here")

As per the work of Heifetz and Linsky (2002), we call these routines "technical" because they ensure the work of the organization marches on the way it always has with improvements around the edges to existing practice.

And then there are routines more like the ones Resnick and Spillane describe, which have the features of the normal routines, but also:

- Build shared understanding of high-quality instruction

- Build capacity of participants to enact or support high-quality instruction through participating in the routine
- Collect data about strategy implementation
- Employ data as feedback to improve the system
- Reduce variation in practice

These adaptive routines are different from the technical ones in that they prepare the organization to change and grow over time. They help make organizations able to shift practice so they can meet evolving conditions and needs.

What is a bit tricky about routines is that the same activity, depending on use, can serve either as a technical or an adaptive routine. Moreover, it's often possible to shift an activity from being a technical routine to an adaptive one, and vice versa. To help ensure your routines are adaptive and thus able to effectively support your Disciplined Strategic Plan, we provide a tool for this purpose (see Figure 6.2).

An example of a routine embedded in schools is the frequent practice of walkthroughs or instructional rounds (City et al., 2009). In some places, these routines are used to build collegiality and to provide an opportunity for teachers to learn from one another. Teachers being observed may receive feedback on their instruction from the observers, and the observers may see instructional practices that they may incorporate into their own instruction. In this way, the walkthroughs meet the criteria of a technical routine—the process is normalized and does provide some opportunities for teachers to enhance their practice.

In contrast, in some of the other districts in which we work, the superintendents are more intentional and more strategic about how they use a routine like this. One district was focused on improving student achievement in mathematics and created an instructional model to be implemented in all math classrooms across the district. This model was accompanied by a plan for professional development for teachers of math at all grade levels. The superintendent instituted instructional rounds for math classrooms: mixed teams of administrators and teachers visited classrooms on a regular schedule and debriefed afterwards using a standardized protocol. This routine of deep discussion about shared observations built understanding about what math instruction ought to look like, built the capacity of participants

Transforming Routines into Adaptive Routines
(to be used to refine existing routines or create new ones)

	Name of Routine:
Logistics	Technical Characteristics (who, what, when, how often, how monitored)
Purpose	How is this routine connected to the overall theory of action/strategy?
Instruction	What is the connection of the routine to a shared understanding of high-quality instruction?
Coherence	How does the routine decrease variation in practice?
Capacity	How does participation in the routine improve the capacity of the participants? (Individual and social learning)
Feedback to the System	How are data collected during the routine employed to improve the theory of action/strategy?
Evalution	How will the efficacy of the routine itself to improve the system be evaluated?

Connecticut Center for School Change. Used with permission.

Figure 6.2 Transforming Routines into Adaptive Routines

to support the math instructional model, and generated data about how the math model was implemented. The result was more than individual teachers deciding or not to change their practice; it was an opportunity to engage in regular assessments of what professional development of all kinds teachers needed. And as the routine was repeated, the variation in implementation of the model from classroom to classroom was reduced. The routine facilitated opportunities for schools to constantly enhance their practice by dynamically responding to shifting student, teacher, and environmental needs. This type of adaptive routine is what you will need to make your Disciplined Strategic Plan a success.

Return to Principles

Remembering again the adage "what gets measured gets done," we return to our principles to ground our monitoring process in what we value most.

Equity

- Accountability is a key condition for equity. Without clear data on what we're doing and the impact it has on children, it will be impossible to direct our efforts toward diminishing inequity and increasing equity.

- The traditional emphasis on outcomes without looking at processes has often allowed for discourses that suggest gaps in performance or disproportionality in other spaces (discipline, special education, etc.) are normal or appropriate. They are not. By focusing our attention on processes and outcomes and centering on equity, we facilitate our ability to identify and address the system- and school-related mechanisms that cause these outcomes, including bias and unequal access to resources.

- Once the data is collected from carefully considered measures, the analysis also needs to attend to issues of equity. One way to achieve this is by disaggregating the data in ways that expose discriminatory patterns that exist in everything from course-taking patterns to differential math achievement scores for different racial groups of students.

- Effective accountability pushes us to not simply quantify what we are or are not doing or accomplishing; it moves us to ask critical questions about whether what we hope to attain is compatible with current systems and structures. For example, if we can't seem to get traction on an intervention aimed at increasing rigor for all students, data from students regarding their relationships with teachers may help us to see whether the issue is both academic and cultural. Disaggregating further, if we were to see that Black and brown students feel less positive than their white peers about these relationships, it would help us to target issues of bias regarding how teachers think about and engage with different groups of students.

Logic

- A strong accountability system facilitates opportunities to consider the effectiveness of an intervention at different points along its implementation. This requires that those engaged in planning carefully consider the order of activities toward full implementation. What will come first? Second? Who will do it? What will happen as a result? Each of these questions needs to be answered and assessed.

- Connected to the above point, the accountability system also needs to attend to the different levels of implementation (that is, adults and students). As already stated, we can't expect to increase student achievement as a result of an intervention teachers haven't fully learned how to implement, or have learned but aren't using in their classrooms.

Coherence

- Measures need to be aligned with your goals and provide information to give insights about potential performance on assessments to which educators and students will ultimately be held accountable.

- Any assessment system should take into consideration and attend to current measurement routines to facilitate alignment and "double-dipping" wherever possible.

- The system also needs to be aligned to some degree with current norms and capacity—if teachers have never shared practice or have traditionally felt a sense of unease with the administration, using measurement tools that immediately require teachers opening their classrooms to everyone and speaking their minds may not be successful. This is not to let people off the hook—you can work up to such measures over time when ready.

Capacity

- An effective accountability system is built on the assumption that a lack of capacity is the root cause of underperformance.

- For an accountability system to support a disciplined strategy, it must focus on uncovering whether and to what degree adequate supports are being provided to facilitate learning and growth at all levels (that is, capacity). It's only when people are given all they need to grow but still do not or refuse to take up the supports provided that accountability should be used as a tool for addressing poor performance at the individual level.

- Adaptive routines aimed at accountability are necessary to support ongoing capacity building across the activities of the plan and the district's and schools' ability to meet new and evolving challenges as the plan progresses.

References

City, E. A., Elmore, R. F., Fiarman, S. E., & Teitel, L. (2009). *Instructional rounds in education*. Cambridge, MA: Harvard Education Press.

Dee, T. S., Jacob, B. A., Hoxby, C. M., & Ladd, H. F. (2010). The impact of No Child Left Behind on students, teachers, and schools [with Comments and Discussion]. *Brookings Papers on Economic Activity*, 149–207.

Elliot, A. J., & Dweck, C. S. (Eds.). (2005). *Handbook of competence and motivation*. New York, NY: Guilford Press.

Elmore, R. F. (2004). *School reform from the inside out: Policy, practice, and performance.* Cambridge, MA: Harvard Education Press

Hannaway, J., & Hamilton, L. (2008). *Performance-based accountability policies: Implications for school and classroom practices.* Washington: Urban Institute and RAND Corporation.

Heifetz, R. A., and M. Linsky. 2002. *Leadership on the line: Staying alive through the dangers of leading.* Boston, MA: Harvard Business School Press.

Resnick, L. B., & Spillane, J. P. (2006). From individual learning to organizational designs for learning. In L. Verschaffel, F. Dochy, M. Boekaerts, & S. Vosniadou (Eds.), *Instructional psychology: Past, present and future trends: Sixteen essays in honor of Erik De Corte* (Advances in Learning and Instruction Series, pp. 259–276). Oxford, UK: Pergamon.

Saultz, A., Murphy, K. M., & Aronson, B. (2016). What can we learn from the Atlanta cheating scandal? *Phi Delta Kappan, 97*(6), 48–52.

7 | Conclusion

In this final chapter, we step away from sharing the why, what, and how of the Disciplined Strategic Planning process to consider its potential impact over time. To do so, we return to Ashburn a couple of years into implementation and provide a quick snapshot of current operations. Specifically, we focus on the district's and its schools' structures and systems and the types of opportunities and outcomes that have become newly available as a result of these efforts. We do this through the eyes of those implicated in the plan: students and educators. Our major themes of Logic, Equity, Capacity, and Coherence are woven throughout.

We present this picture as an aspiration. It assumes that Ashburn's Disciplined Strategic Plan remained the anchor for decision-making in the district over time. Even when difficult times came—COVID-19 closures, budget cuts, external policy pressures—they stuck to their core vision and mission and modified the plan only when it was necessary and only in ways that continued to best serve their students. At the same time, the plan and implementation existed in a fluid state such that implementation was informed by and responsive to changing needs. As we discuss below for each stakeholder group, this would have meant the creation and ongoing modification of institutional routines to support the continual identification of need (monitoring) as well as a willingness and capacity to infuse differentiated resources to meet evolving needs. In other words, we assume they did what the plan suggested.

Students

Let's start with Ashburn's students. Our aspirations for them, of course, are that they all leave Ashburn able to follow whatever path they choose because they've gained the knowledge, skills, and other characteristics they, their teachers, and their caregivers agreed are important for them to be successful (the portrait of the graduate). While they're in school, we hope they have equal and equitable access to rigorous coursework, see reflections of themselves in the curriculum, and work with adults who make them feel valued. Policies related to issues such as behavior, discipline, and dress code don't inflict disproportionately negative impacts on students of color or other groups who have traditionally been marginalized. Students with specialized learning needs receive the support they need from their teachers. When students question school rules and their fairness, adults meaningfully engage with them about these questions and treat students as active co-constructors of their schooling experience

In keeping with the plan's emphasis on logic and coherence, the variability in students' experiences within and across schools has gradually decreased. Instead, students understand and can articulate at a developmentally appropriate level how what they learn today connects to their past learnings and what they will learn in the future. As students go from class to class and grade to grade, instructional strategies are repeated and extended. Ashburn's students have an ongoing "toolbox" from which they can consistently draw. Students, too, know the learning habits they need to be successful in Ashburn schools. Finally, if a student moves to a different school in the district, they can pick up where they left off with relative ease.

Teachers

Teachers in Ashburn schools are now part of an educational infrastructure that builds teachers' capacity to meet the instructional goals articulated in the portrait of the graduate. The district developed a definition of high-quality instruction they believe will help get their students where they need to be each year and by graduation. This definition prioritizes instructional practices that are highest leverage—the ones most likely to get students to realize the portrait of the graduate and to have the greatest effect on previously lower-achieving students while raising achievement overall. Teachers have embraced this orientation and coupled it with other efforts to identify and address their and others' discrimination and bias as well as enhance their practice.

Teachers understand that equity is a foundational value of the district and that the commitment to see the work through an equity lens is real. They know what is expected of them, and they feel supported in making access, experiences, and outcomes for students more equitable. The district strategy makes it clear that leadership is accountable for producing equitable opportunities and outcomes for students and is willing to act regarding policies and practices to make this so. With the support of books, best practices, and difficult but well-facilitated discussions, teachers have worked hard to examine and undo their discriminatory views, recognize and address such discrimination when it occurs, and better understand the strengths their students bring to their classrooms. They have also taken action by shifting curricular resources so they better reflect and connect with students' experiences.

To support such shifts and new learning, all teachers belong to at least one learning community that meets weekly. During their meetings, teachers review the results of their collective attempts to improve their instructional practice. They use the information they collected on what worked well and what didn't to decide what they'll try next to improve their instruction. These interventions are aligned with their best guess as to what is going to be most effective in improving student learning and ensuring equitable access and outcomes for all.

The work of learning communities is the most prevalent routine for improving instruction, but other routines have also had an effect on enhancing practice, if less directly. Teachers and administrators from across the district, for example, are involved in regularly scheduled visits to sample classrooms. This provides participants with a broader picture of how the strategy for improving instruction is unfolding across the district. Teachers also visit one another's classrooms more often and with a clear sense of purpose and improvement goals. The data collected from these visits is used to inform coaching and other professional development teachers receive.

From the teachers' perspective, the direction the district is taking regarding improvement is apparent, and they can see that initiatives are evidence-based. The district leadership team participates in visits to classrooms throughout the district and engages with teachers around data. Leadership's recommendations feel connected to these discussions and thus clearer and more logical. This is a far cry from the "initiative churn" teachers were used to, when the focus of the district changed from year to year and teachers never felt that they had a chance to reach mastery in any given new initiative. The routines in which teachers participate regularly to build their capacity also build coherence; teachers feel connected to the vision and mission of the district, but they also feel connected to one another in new and stronger ways.

Mezzanine Leaders

Mezzanine leaders, like teachers, benefit from the increased logic of the district strategy. Perhaps the biggest impact of the new planning process on Ashburn's coaches and teacher leaders is that their roles are so much clearer. The mezzanine leaders had always felt valued—indeed, they were inclined to believe the district would implode without them—but they were underutilized. In the absence of either a clear direction as to their responsibilities or a shared understanding of what good instruction should look like, mezzanine leaders' work with teachers frequently devolved into an extended negotiation where the leaders tried to provide feedback and classroom support and teachers pushed back on or resisted such efforts. Often administrators were no help because they, too, felt the lack of clear direction from the district. As a result of the planning process, the district has become more coherent. The lines about what mezzanine leaders should do and why are clearer, and they are much more effective as a result.

Moreover, because the expectations of the mezzanine leaders are clearer, the needs for their professional growth are also clearer, and the mezzanine leaders receive more useful professional development. They also have greater and better leverage to engage with teachers in purposeful ways oriented toward enhancing instruction. They visit teachers in their classrooms and coach, coteach, model instruction, and everything else in between based on the teachers' needs. These efforts are connected to the now-articulated idea that teachers' learning needs to be attended to before student outcomes improve.

The mezzanine leaders were selected in part because they were committed to equity. This commitment, however, was not always enough to allow them to play a significant role in creating more equitable access, experiences, or outcomes for all students. A goal that comes down to the personal advocacy of a few educators within a district is not truly a systemic approach. The more explicit approach to equity contained in the district's strategy made it clear to everyone that the mezzanine leaders were enacting an organizational, rather than a personal, value. They also received training and resources about how to engage in and facilitate difficult conversations about discrimination and bias. This has sometimes meant pointing out problems with well-established or even beloved traditions (think a mascot depicting indigenous peoples in a racist or stereotyped way). Because of the district vision, they feel more emboldened to bring up such issues and are supported when they do so.

Principals

Under the district's Disciplined Strategic Plan, the principals' role regarding capacity remains transparent; there is a plan for building capacity for instruction aligned to the district's model for high-quality instruction. Principals understand what it is and how it fits within the larger strategy. They no longer feel they are individual-level arbiters of quality when it comes to instruction through their role as evaluators. While they can be responsive to teachers' needs, they need not be the sole purveyors of professional development to teachers. Instead, it's clear that their responsibility is to ensure mezzanine leaders and teachers get the support they need to build their knowledge and skills. Principals ensure teachers' access to the resources and structures they need to be successful.

Just as teachers and the mezzanine leaders appreciate that the district now recognizes that issues of equity need to be attended to across all levels of the system, principals understand that their role regarding equity has increased. When teachers, parents, or students come to them with concerns about whether and how certain policies are equitable, they no longer feel the need to be defensive or to protect traditions for fear of more powerful constituency groups going over the principals' heads to get what they want from the district. Policies and structures that were once treated as untouchable are now up for discussion and debate. The focus on equity has also allowed principals, with training and support, to feel they could engage in these conversations with teachers more deeply and in ways that have helped bring more justice to everything from the discipline policy to the assignment of teachers.

Principals have embraced the logic of the plan, and specifically the idea that there is a stepwise or temporal quality to the introduction, implementation, and outcomes of interventions. They are inclined less toward treating teachers as difficult or unwilling to learn, and more toward thinking about how they might best support teachers across their learning trajectory, differentiating support when needed. They now push for using data at all levels of implementation to both model such behavior for teachers and to ensure that their decisions are grounded in data and thus clear and transparent to all.

Principals deeply appreciate being part of a through-line regarding instructional and strategic improvement that goes all the way from the central office to the classroom. It makes it easier for them to communicate with teachers and the school community. They no longer must engage in the mental gymnastics of figuring out how district and school policies with different and often conflicting assumptions and goals fit together or having to convince others that these policies make sense. Rather than feeling a diminishing sense of autonomy, principals actually feel more empowered and part of district decision-making. By transparently defining the ends (goals) and the overarching strategy, it gives those at the local level more power to control the means (processes) aligned with the specific contextual needs.

Central Office

Equity is the centerpiece of all communication and policies. When decisions are made, it is clear, through ongoing conversation with multiple stakeholders, that the potential impacts on different groups—and vulnerable populations in particular—have been thoroughly discussed and attended to. As already highlighted in the experiences of students, teachers, and leaders, the district now provides ongoing training and resources that promote antiracist and antidiscriminatory practices throughout the system. This includes district staff turning inward and reflecting together and individually about these issues.

Additionally, the district now engages in regular audits of current policies and practices and continues to critique how they may uphold the status quo. This moved those in the district to make substantive changes to a number of policies (access to AP classes, discipline and behavioral codes, class placement, etc.). They have also worked to influence teachers' everyday actions as they engage with students and in their teaching and learning (embracing asset-based orientations, using more representative materials, engaging with parents as partners). The district was also willing to take and stand by an approach focused on distributing resources where they were needed more (i.e., equitably) rather than evenly regardless of need (i.e., equally).

The superintendent ensures that the logic and the coherence of the plan are reinforced through several mechanisms. Her regularly scheduled conversations with principals are centered on how routines are being used to build capacity and to generate data that cast light on how effective the strategy is and how to improve it. Central office staff are now regularly out in the schools, participating in classroom walkthroughs and engaging in conversations with those on the ground about the efficacy and effectiveness of current supports and structures. As a result, district employees take a service orientation toward their work, helping educators and families navigate the system rather than putting up barriers to access.

Budget conversations, too, are directly linked to the plan, and discussions about what is being spent and why are clearly aligned with the goals. When budgets were tight, this sometimes meant pet programs or popular activities only loosely aligned with district goals were cut to save coaching positions and the ability to ensure there was enough coverage for teachers to meet together regularly. When harder times came, the district was able to prioritize and make the best decisions possible given a no-win situation. Such decisions were difficult but were public and clear, which made it easier for everyone to understand. This new transparency and additional communication have also made it possible for more people to be involved in giving feedback and in decision-making. And now that there was greater alignment between schools in terms of materials and approaches, the district had an easier time negotiating with external vendors to get a fair price at scale for needed resources.

The district also takes a more proactive stance, with the board and the state sharing the good things the district is doing and highlighting the practices and routines that make these successes possible. The office now feels empowered to push back when these external entities mandate reforms or initiatives misaligned with the district's goals. Finally, and to keep up with the schools' evolving needs and growth, the district has also invested in building its capacity to meet schools' needs. The district focused more on coaching than compliance activities and worked to ensure that when the district asks things of the principals, the activities are connected to their core work of instructional leadership and continuous improvement.

Concluding Thoughts

As this is a book about planning, we steer clear of discussing or describing implementation, since the idea of execution or getting things done is the subject of other books by other authors. Instead, we focus on reinventing the planning process from a compliance activity to a meaningful and disciplined process anchored in clear principles and oriented toward continuous improvement. One of the things we've tried to convey throughout this book is that planning is not a "one and done" activity. Planning is continuous in the same way that improvement is continuous—it's never done, and it requires ongoing attention to be sustained.

Our primary goal is to liberate educators from a planning process that does very little to improve the opportunities, experiences, and outcomes for students. We've worked with so many leaders who recognize that the plans they develop don't actually drive the work of improvement on a day-to-day basis. We wanted to address this and provide a beneficial alternative.

Of course, one of the difficulties of a more effective planning process is that real, deep, and disciplined planning takes energy and time over the course of the whole plan (until the goals are met)—time and energy those in charge of planning often feel they cannot spare. While we would love to be able to say "if you just do this one thing...," it's unfortunately not possible. The work is what makes the plan worthwhile. It's what can help you meet the goals that have long felt too audacious or out of reach to come true. We have to be all in. At the same time, "those who have a million priorities have none," so we leave you with what we view as the most important core ideas of the disciplined planning process.

- The principles should guide your plan. Given that much of the early stages of plan development are about uncovering strengths but also weaknesses, a light touch or timid approach is a surefire way to fail. Like the work of leadership, this process generally takes courage and a willingness to anchor oneself in principles even when it's inconvenient or difficult. Be brave and know that the only way to get different outcomes in terms of planning and continuous improvement is to do things differently.

- Don't worry about what your plan looks like. It can be a professionally produced website, a humble collection of Google docs, or a bunch of sticky notes on a whiteboard. What matters is that you think deeply about what it will take to realize your aspirations for students and create a map for getting there. What the final product looks like is a technical question that can be delegated. The heavy cognitive lifting is where you should put your energy.

- Despite what you may have been told, process trumps product. The effort of creating a long and involved plan is squandered when you don't invest in developing and then actually enacting routines to ensure the work of the plan is done and that data are gathered along the way to help make the process better. This doesn't mean that you shouldn't have vision and goals—the work won't matter if you don't know where you're going—but knowing where you're going is not enough to get you there.

- Don't make any assumptions about what people know about high-quality instruction.

- Invest heavily in building capacity in educators. They, like your students, require support and compassion to learn new things.

- Don't think you can browbeat people into doing what you want. Communicate very clearly what you mean by accountability. It should mean that people have to try. It shouldn't mean the threat of punishment if they're not immediately successful.

- Routines, routines, routines. Our belief in the power of well-constructed routines is reiterated throughout the book, but we just want to emphasize one last time that one of the most effective ways of bringing your strategic plan to life is to embody the work in high-frequency routines.

Armed with these core ideas and the Disciplined Strategic Planning tools in this book, you should feel ready and able to engage in planning in new and more powerful ways. We face many challenges ahead, and it will be new ways of thinking and working that will allow us to better meet them. Learning together, we can make planning an engine for continuous improvement and, in doing so, make our schools more just, more effective, and more positive for the adults working in them and the young people and communities they serve.